CW00766465

BLACKPOOL TRAMWAYS 1933-66

Stephen Lockwood

Series editor Robert J Harley

MP Middleton Press

Front Cover:

This is a typically busy scene on the Promenade near Central Station with streamlined trams in abundance. English Electric railcoach 215 is approaching the three track section near the Tower, where the preceding Coronation car is negotiating the points, passing an open boat car. The illuminated crown on top of the shelter in the centre distance indicates that this view dates from Coronation year, 1953. (W.J. Haynes)

Back Cover:

The last tramcars built for Blackpool for 24 years were the ten trailers delivered in 1960. These were matched with ten rebuilt railcoaches to form 'Twin car' units. Two of these sets are seen at the Little Bispham turning circle on 24th October 1966, with the Irish Sea in the background. Trailer car T6 (686), coupled to railcoach 276 (676) is in the foreground. In the background, in the newer livery of half green and cream, is T2 (682) coupled to 272 (672), one of the seven 'Twin car' sets that were modified to be permanently coupled, with a driver's cab provided in the trailer. 276 and T6 would be converted to this layout in 1969. (L.G.Sidwell)

Cover colours:

These represent the cars of the period.

PublishedAugust 2008

ISBN 978 1 906008 34 5

Design Deborah Esher

Published by
Middleton Press
Easebourne Lane
Midhurst
West Sussex
GU29 9AZ
Tel: 01730 813169
Fax: 01730 812601
Email: info@middletonpress.co.uk
www.middletonpress.co.uk

Printed & bound by Biddles Ltd, Kings Lynn

CONTENTS

The Journey

The Streamliners

INTRODUCTION AND ACKNOWLEDGEMENTS

Blackpool's trams require no introduction. Like the town itself, the tramway is iconic and a 'national treasure'. Blackpool without its trams is an unthinkable concept. The town introduced Britain's first electric street tramway in 1885. Between 1962 and 1992 it was Britain's only electric street tramway. It is a transport system that can move the sheer numbers of people visiting the resort during the long summer season, lengthened by the autumn Illuminations. It is able to do this because of the foresight of the municipal planners, who constructed wide promenades incorporating a paved track for the trams, separated from other road traffic. Added to this was the massive modernisation of the tram fleet in the years before the Second World War, which ensured that riding on the trams was as pleasurable, fast and comfortable as possible as well as ensuring that the trams were indispensable to Blackpool.

This album is being published to commemorate the 75th anniversary of the entry into service of the first of these streamlined trams in 1933. It is fitting that this anniversary falls in 2008, which is proving to be another vital year in the tramway's long history. This year has seen the re-opening of the tramway after an unprecedented winter closure for track rebuilding. These works have produced the most comprehensive changes to the overall track layout for over sixty years. Added to this, 2008 is the year that the tramway finally affirmed its long term future, with the confirmation of funding to produce the necessary renewals including the procurement of a new generation of low floor articulated trams.

The aim of this album is to show the tramway, route by route in the period between 1933 and 1966, concentrating on the streamlined cars that entered service up to 1960. I have chosen photographs which, in the main, have not been published before or have not previously had a wide circulation. To assist readers, I have included in the captions, where possible, both the original and post-1968 fleet number of the cars. Readers requiring more details of Blackpool's tram history are directed to the comprehensive review of the pre-1933 fleet by Abell and McLauchlin, and also the historical volumes by Brian Turner and Steve Palmer.

I am grateful for the support of all those photographers, and suppliers of prints, who have allowed their collections to be used. Any uncredited views are from my own collection.

Thanks for assistance are also given to: Steve Burd and Bryan Lindop of Blackpool Transport Services; the staff of Blackpool Central Library Local Studies Section; Roger Smith for drawing the excellent track map and Peter Cardno for reading my text and making appropriate suggestions for improvement. Norman Langridge has kindly proofread the text. As ever, my wife Eileen has supported me throughout this project. She knows Blackpool's trams well, having spent many hours with me riding on them.

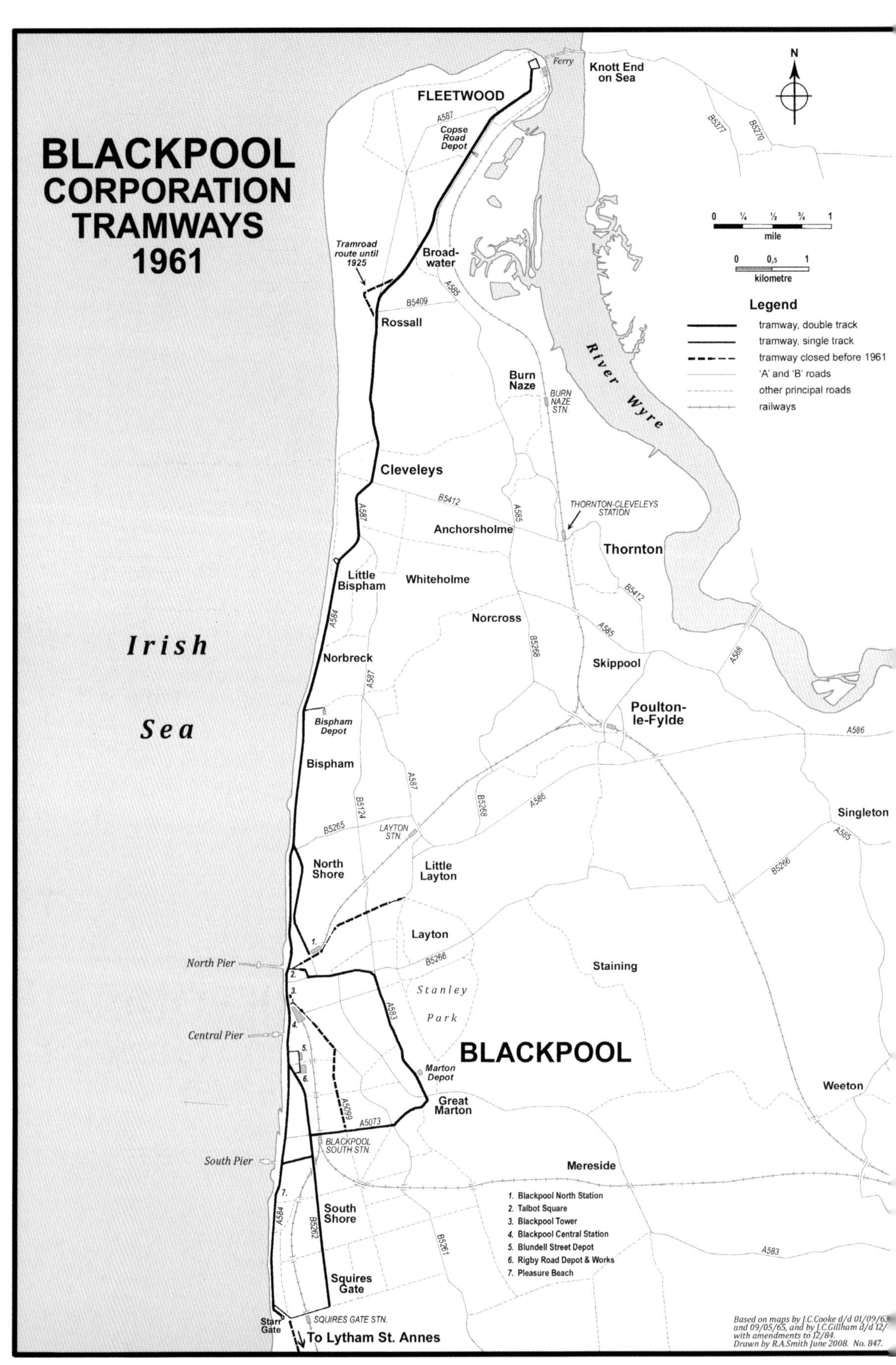

BLACKPOOL CORPORATION TRAMWAYS 1961
N
0 ¼ ½ ¾ 1
mile
0 0,5 1
kilometre
Legend
tramway, double track
tramway, single track
tramway closed before 1961
'A' and 'B' roads
other principal roads
railways
Irish Sea
River Wyre
FLEETWOOD
Ferry
Knott End on Sea
Copse Road Depot
Tramroad route until 1925
Broad-water
Rossall
Burn Naze
BURN NAZE STN.
Cleveleys
Anchorsholme
THORNTON-CLEVELEYS STATION
Thornton
Little Bispham
Whiteholme
Norcross
Norbreck
Skippool
Bispham Depot
Poulton-le-Fylde
Bispham
Singleton
LAYTON STN.
North Shore
Little Layton
Layton
North Pier
Staining
Stanley Park
Central Pier
BLACKPOOL
Marton Depot
Great Marton
Weeton
BLACKPOOL SOUTH STN.
South Pier
Mereside
South Shore
Squires Gate
SQUIRES GATE STN.
Starr Gate
To Lytham St. Annes
A587
B5377
B5270
A585
B5409
B5412
A584
B5268
A588
A586
B5124
B5265
B5266
A583
A5099
A5073
B5262
B5261
1. Blackpool North Station
2. Talbot Square
3. Blackpool Tower
4. Blackpool Central Station
5. Blundell Street Depot
6. Rigby Road Depot & Works
7. Pleasure Beach
Based on maps by J.C.Cooke d/d 01/09/63 and 09/05/65, and by J.C.Gillham d/d 12/ with amendments to 12/84.
Drawn by R.A.Smith June 2008. No. 847.

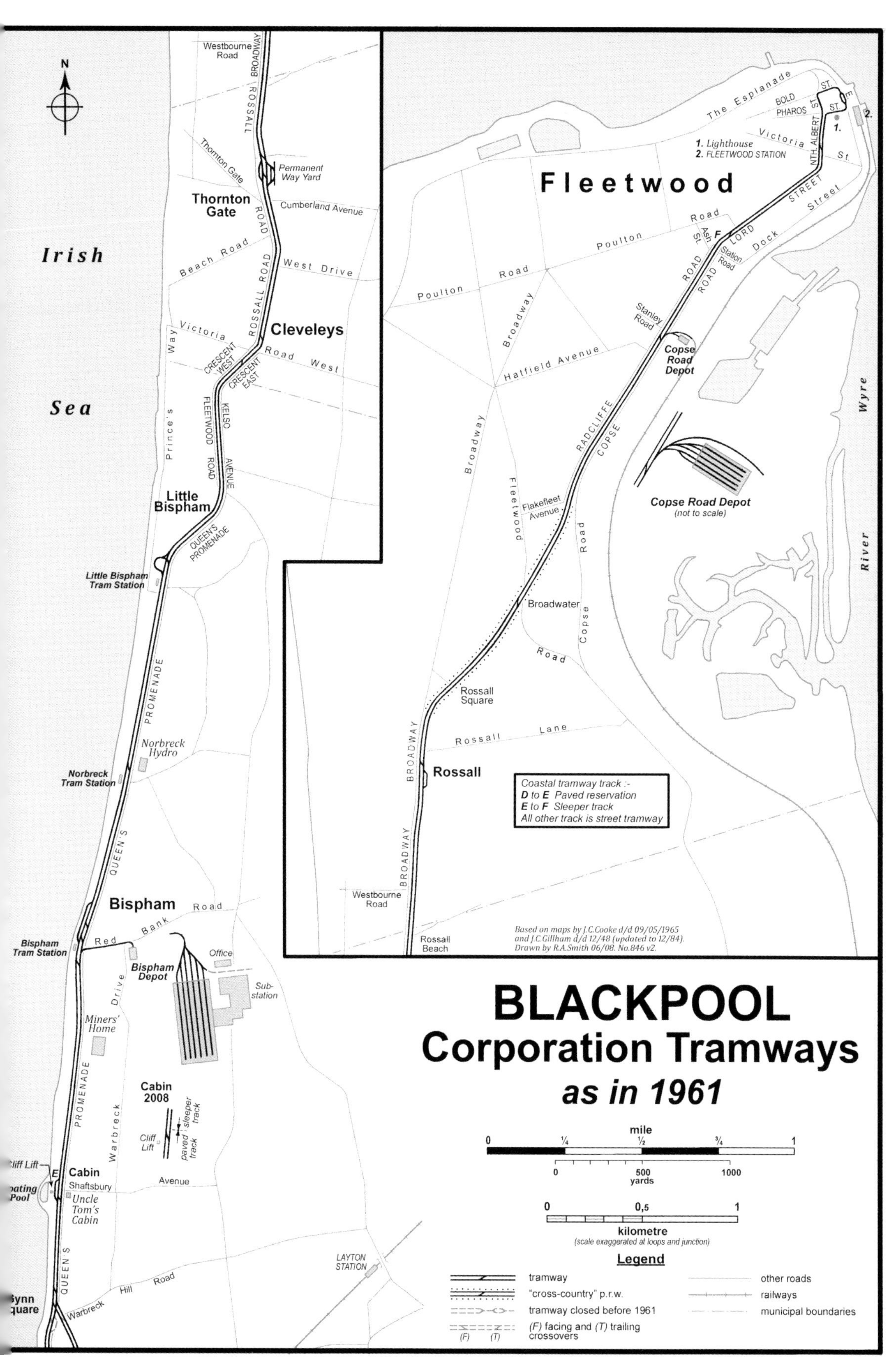
BLACKPOOL
Corporation Tramways
as in 1961
Irish Sea
Fleetwood
Westbourne Road
Rossall Broadway
Thornton Gate
Permanent Way Yard
Cumberland Avenue
Beach Road
West Drive
Rossall Road
Cleveleys
Victoria Road West
Crescent West
Crescent East
Prince's Way
Fleetwood Road
Kelso Avenue
Little Bispham
Queen's Promenade
Little Bispham Tram Station
Norbreck Hydro
Norbreck Tram Station
Bispham
Red Bank Road
Bispham Tram Station
Bispham Depot
Office
Sub-station
Miners' Home
Drive
Warbreck
Cabin 2008
Cliff Lift
paved
sleeper track
Cliff Lift
Cabin
Shaftsbury Avenue
Uncle Tom's Cabin
Boating Pool
Warbreck Hill Road
Gynn Square
Layton Station
The Esplanade
Bold St.
Pharos St.
Victoria St.
Nth. Albert St.
1. Lighthouse
2. FLEETWOOD STATION
Lord Street
Dock Street
Poulton Road
Ash St.
Station Road
Broadway
Stanley Road
Copse Road Depot
Hatfield Avenue
Radcliffe Road
Copse Road
Copse Road Depot
(not to scale)
River Wyre
Fleetwood Road
Flakefleet Avenue
Broadwater
Rossall Square
Rossall Lane
Rossall
Coastal tramway track :-
D to E Paved reservation
E to F Sleeper track
All other track is street tramway
Rossall Beach
Based on maps by J.C.Cooke d/d 09/05/1965
and J.C.Gillham d/d 12/48 (updated to 12/84).
Drawn by R.A.Smith 06/08. No.846 v2.
mile
0 ¼ ½ ¾ 1
0 500 1000
yards
0 0,5 1
kilometre
(scale exaggerated at loops and junction)
Legend
tramway
"cross-country" p.r.w.
tramway closed before 1961
(F) facing and (T) trailing crossovers
other roads
railways
municipal boundaries

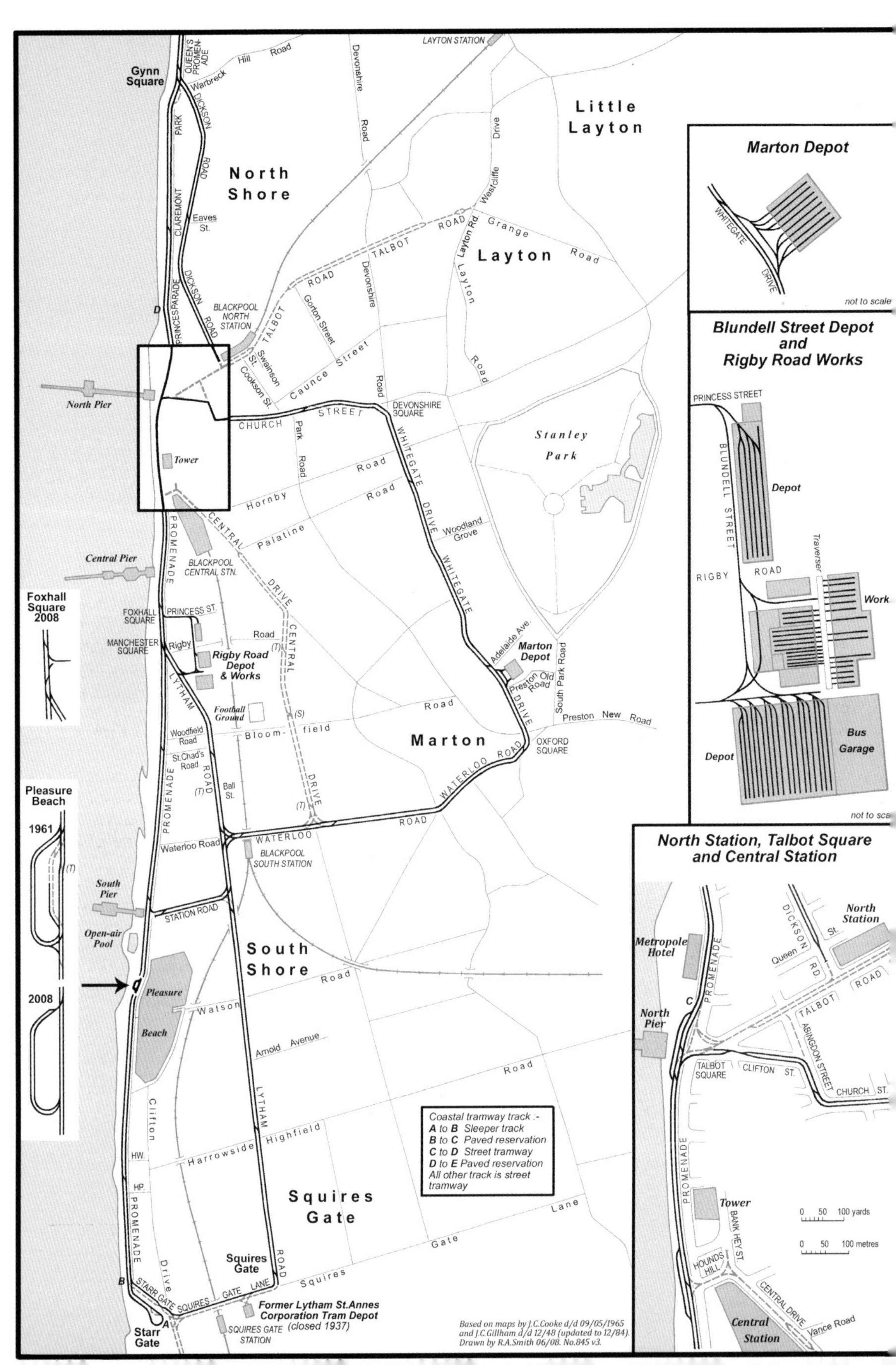

Gynn Square
QUEEN'S PROMENADE
Warbreck Hill Road
LAYTON STATION
Devonshire Road
Little Layton
PARK
DICKSON ROAD
North Shore
CLAREMONT
Eaves St.
Drive
Westcliffe
Grange Road
Layton Rd.
Layton
Layton Road
TALBOT ROAD
Devonshire
Gorton Street
PRINCES PARADE
D
BLACKPOOL NORTH STATION
Swainson St.
Cookson St.
Caunce Street
Road
North Pier
DEVONSHIRE SQUARE
CHURCH STREET
Park Road
Tower
WHITEGATE DRIVE
Hornby Road
Stanley Park
Palatine Road
Woodland Grove
CENTRAL DRIVE
PROMENADE
Central Pier
BLACKPOOL CENTRAL STN.
Foxhall Square 2008
FOXHALL SQUARE
PRINCESS ST.
MANCHESTER SQUARE
Rigby
Road
(T)
Rigby Road Depot & Works
Adelaide Ave.
Marton Depot
Preston Old Road
South Park Road
LYTHAM
Football Ground
(S)
Woodfield Road
Bloomfield
Marton
Preston New Road
OXFORD SQUARE
St.Chad's Road
ROAD
Ball St.
WATERLOO ROAD
Pleasure Beach
1961
Waterloo Road
BLACKPOOL SOUTH STATION
South Pier
STATION ROAD
Open-air Pool
South Shore
Pleasure Beach
Watson Road
2008
Arnold Avenue
Road
Clifton Drive
HW.
HP.
Harrowside
Highfield
LYTHAM ROAD
Squires Gate
Lane
Gate
Squires
Squires Gate
B
STARR GATE
SQUIRES GATE LANE
A
Starr Gate
Former Lytham St.Annes Corporation Tram Depot (closed 1937)
SQUIRES GATE STATION
Coastal tramway track :-
A to B Sleeper track
B to C Paved reservation
C to D Street tramway
D to E Paved reservation
All other track is street tramway
Based on maps by J.C.Cooke d/d 09/05/1965 and J.C.Gillham d/d 12/48 (updated to 12/84). Drawn by R.A.Smith 06/08. No.845 v3.
Marton Depot
WHITEGATE DRIVE
not to scale
Blundell Street Depot and Rigby Road Works
PRINCESS STREET
BLUNDELL STREET
Depot
Traverser
RIGBY ROAD
Works
Depot
Bus Garage
not to scale
North Station, Talbot Square and Central Station
Metropole Hotel
PROMENADE
DICKSON RD.
Queen St.
North Station
TALBOT ROAD
North Pier
C
ABINGDON STREET
TALBOT SQUARE
CLIFTON ST.
CHURCH ST.
Tower
BANK HEY ST.
HOUNDS HILL
CENTRAL DRIVE
Central Station
Vance Road
0 50 100 yards
0 50 100 metres

GEOGRAPHICAL SETTING

The seaside resort of Blackpool is the principal town on The Fylde peninsula, 15 miles/24km west of Preston. It began to grow as a seaside retreat in the 18th century, but it was after the coming of the railway in 1846 that the modern resort, noted for 'fresh air and fun', began to flourish. The North Pier was opened in 1863 and the Tower, 518 feet/157.8 metres high, followed in 1894. In the first half of the 20th century, whole communities throughout Lancashire would descend on Blackpool for their 'Wakes Week' holiday. Eight miles north of Blackpool, lying on the mouth of the River Wyre, is Fleetwood, founded as a fishing port and famous for its traditional covered market.

HISTORICAL BACKGROUND

Britain's first electric street tramway, the Blackpool Electric Tramway Co Ltd, was inaugurated in Blackpool on 29th September 1885. This was a line of almost two miles in length, running between Cocker Square, just north of North Pier, along the Promenade southwards to Dean Street, which was near the site of the later Victoria Pier (opened in 1893). Designed and managed by Michael Holroyd Smith, the Halifax based electrical engineer, the system was powered by the conduit system, with a central 'slot' in-between the running rails. Ten open top double deck cars were operated. The Company was taken over by Blackpool Corporation in 1892, and the tramway system has been in municipal ownership ever since.

The tramway was extended in 1895, when a line opened branching off the Promenade at Manchester Square running along Lytham Road as far as Station Road. A separate line ran from Station Road along the remainder of Lytham Road to Squires Gate. Initially worked by horse traction, this latter stretch was leased in 1896 to the Blackpool, St Annes and Lytham Tramway Company and operated as a through service from Station Road to Lytham using gas powered trams. A further extension to the Lytham Road conduit tramway occurred in 1897 when an extension along Station Road to the Promenade at Victoria (later South) Pier was brought into use, as well as a short extension of the Promenade tramway to the same point, allowing a circular service to operate.

The next and very significant development was the opening in 1898 of the Blackpool and Fleetwood Electric Tramroad. This overhead electric tramway ran for 8½ miles/13.6km between Talbot Road railway station (later Blackpool North), via Gynn Square, Bispham, and Cleveleys to Fleetwood. Apart from street running at either end of the service, the route was on a private right of way. This was the first overhead electric street tramway in Blackpool.

The conduit tramway, being experimental, was beset by several problems. Sea water ingress and the general salt and sand atmosphere of the Promenade caused frequent power failures, resulting in the cars being hauled by horses for protracted periods. The introduction of the Fleetwood tramway with its overhead power supply encouraged the Corporation to convert its lines to this system during 1899, and the following year, to open an extension northwards along the North Promenade from Cocker Square to Gynn Square. Here passengers could interchange from the Promenade cars onto the Fleetwood trams.

The earliest years of the twentieth century saw the Corporation introduce trams on inland services. In 1901, lines opened along Central Drive and from Talbot Square to Marton, connecting to the Lytham Road tramway at Royal Oak. The following year the Talbot Square to Layton Square service started, running along Talbot Road. The Promenade line was not neglected. By 1905, the line between North Pier and Victoria Pier, along the Central Promenade, had been moved onto reserved track on a much widened Promenade, a provision that much later was to ensure the tramway's survival. In addition, a short extension at the southern end brought the tracks to a new terminus near to the Pleasure Beach, where an impressive four track terminal layout was provided for use by the end loading Dreadnought double deck bogie cars.

From 1905, the Lytham trams, now electrified and owned by Lytham St Annes Council, were allowed to run through into Blackpool, although not along the Promenade, terminating at either Manchester Square or Central Station.

In 1920, Blackpool Corporation purchased outright the Blackpool and Fleetwood Tramroad Company, with its lengthy route to Fleetwood. This action began a process of overall modernisation of the system. By 1924, the tracks along the North Promenade and the former tramroad up the hill from the Gynn to the Cabin had been placed on paved reserved track and a new track layout opened at Gynn Square connecting the Promenade and Tramroad systems. This allowed the extension of the Promenade trams and by 1926 the Dreadnoughts and Standards were working as far as Bispham. In addition, a service using former Tramroad cars was started from the Pleasure Beach through to Fleetwood. The blue Lytham trams also benefited, being allowed to run along the Central Promenade from Manchester Square to Talbot Square in 1923.

There were developments at the other end of the Promenade service – an extension beyond the Pleasure Beach along the New South Promenade to Starr Gate came into use in 1927. The following year a track connection was made using a short stretch of street track at Clifton Drive onto the Lytham system which allowed the blue cars onto the Promenade from here, running right through to Gynn Square, with alternate cars operating via Lytham Road.

By 1932, Blackpool was running 167 cars over 40 miles/64km of track. The Transport Department took stock, and needed to renew much of its fleet, some of it inherited from the Tramroad company, as well as the ageing, and potentially unsafe Dreadnought cars.

A Five Year Modernisation Plan was drawn up covering both trams and buses and a new manager, Walter Luff, appointed to implement it. Sensing an opportunity, tram manufacturer English Electric offered Blackpool a revolutionary design of streamlined centre entrance single deck car. Entering service in June 1933, the prototype car was seen as the first of a fleet that would rejuvenate the Promenade and Fleetwood tramway. Further cars were ordered immediately, and followed quickly by open top and covered double deck versions, as well as a batch of open single deck cars. To house this fleet of 84 streamlined cars, a new depot was opened in 1935.

A further facet of the Modernisation Plan came to fruition at the end of the 1936 summer season, when the Layton and Central Drive tram routes were abandoned and replaced by buses. Another reduction in tram operation occurred in the following April, when the Lytham blue cars ceased running. To fill the resultant gap in the number of trams on the Promenade more streamlined trams, this time built by Brush, entered service during 1937.

By the outbreak of war, Blackpool had put into service 116 streamlined trams and virtually all the oldest cars had been withdrawn. World War II halted further progress. The early years of peace saw the reconstruction of the only surviving purely inland route to Marton, and railcoaches were allocated to the service by the end of the 1940s. Twenty five new single deck cars, wider and longer than the pre-war versions, came in the early 1950s to operate the Promenade to Fleetwood service. By 1959, there were 164 trams running over 35 miles/56km of track and carrying 34 million passengers that year.

In the late 1950s, the policy began to change and operating economies were being sought. Following an experiment, ten of the original design of railcoach were rebuilt and used with a similar number of newly built trailer cars to form 'Twin car' sets, considerably increasing capacity on the Promenade services. The tramways away from the Promenade then came under scrutiny, and at the end of each season in October, they were closed one by one, starting with the Lytham Road service to Squires Gate on 29th October 1961, then the Marton route on 28th October 1962, and finally the number 1 service along Dickson Road to North Station on 27th October 1963. The following winter no trams ran in Blackpool, although a shuttle service was maintained between Cleveleys and Fleetwood. This was one economy not repeated.

Further cost cutting came about in the early 1970s, when the remaining original English Electric railcoaches were totally rebuilt into trams able to be operated without a guard. These One Man Operated (OMO) cars, as they were then known, took over the basic year round Fleetwood service for the next decade or so, being joined by two double deck OMO cars, again rebuilt from

1930s streamlined cars, in 1979 and 1982 respectively. Eight brand new trams came in the mid-1980s just as the tramway celebrated its centenary on 29th September 1985. A year later, the enforced deregulation of bus services meant that the trams, but not the track, became owned by a company, Blackpool Transport Services Ltd, which was wholly owned by Blackpool Borough Council.

As the tramway approached the Millennium, there was growing concern about the investment necessary to renew the electrical supply, the tracks and the cars. In 1995 the electrical supply, including the traction poles and overhead wiring, was renewed between Starr Gate and Thornton Gate. Into the new century, the emphasis was on the tracks. From late 2002, and throughout the 2003 season, double deckers were banned from running to Fleetwood due to the state of the tramroad track at the outer end of the route. Capacity on the service was maintained by using the 'Twin car' sets on the timetabled service for the first time ever. Complete rebuilding of the defective track brought the brought the double deck cars back to the route in 2004. Since then, major track rebuilding has taken place during the winter months at strategic locations of the system. This culminated in the winter of 2007/8 when, for the first time in its history, the tramway closed completely to allow track rebuilding to be undertaken on several sites including a considerable alteration to the track layout at the Pleasure Beach.

Although this renewal work will ensure the short to medium term future of the line, agencies have for many years been endeavouring to identify enough funding to guarantee the tramway's long term future. Finally, in February 2008, 75 years after Walter Luff embarked on the previous Blackpool tramway revolution, the Department of Transport confirmed that the tramway would receive a total of £85 million, made up of £60 million from central Government and the remainder from Lancashire County and Blackpool Borough Councils. The plan included the provision of a fleet of 16 low floor articulated trams together with a new depot in which to house them; the upgrade of tram stops to be fully accessible, and the completion of the outstanding track and electricity supply renewals.

The major tram stops on the Blackpool and Fleetwood Tramroad between Bispham and Fleetwood have always been referred to as 'Stations' and some are signed as such.

Blackpool's tramway is operated by Blackpool Transport Services Ltd, trading as Metro Coastlines. Rigby Road Blackpool FY1 5DD. www.blackpooltransport.com Managing Director Steven Burd.

Boat car carries royal passenger

On Friday 27th June 2008, the 1935 prototype streamlined open boat car 600 (formerly 225), carried Camilla, Duchess of Cornwall for a short journey between Victoria Street and North Pier. The Duchess was visiting Blackpool during Veterans Week. The car was repainted in its original 1930s livery and suitably decorated with Union Flag bunting along the side handrails, crossed flags over each tow bracket, and circular Union Flags on the discs in the trolley tower. Red, white and blue triangular bunting graced the trolley pole and similar coloured lamps along the lights strung between the trolley tower and each corner of the car.

Special permission from Buckingham Palace was obtained to name the car 'Duchess of Cornwall' and nameplates have been fitted above each entrance below the destination indicators. The named and decorated car was kept under armed police guard prior to the Royal visit. The two crew members for the Royal ride were both service veterans and the Duchess presented them both with special commemorative Veterans badges.

Local tramway interest organisations:

Fylde Tramway Society: Membership Secretary Nick Entwistle 23 Norkeed Court Queens Promenade Blackpool FY5 1PU

Lancastrian Transport Trust: Membership Secretary James Millington 267 Hawes Side Lane South Shore Blackpool FY4 5AQ. www.ltt.org.uk

BEFORE THE STREAMLINER REVOLUTION

1. The 'Circular Tour' by open toastrack tram was one of the major holiday delights in Blackpool before the second world war. 24 of these cars were purchased from 1911, being used on the tours and Promenade work. Such was the demand that a further six slightly smaller cars joined the fleet in 1927. The Tour started and finished at Talbot Square, operating south along the Promenade and then traversing the Marton route in an anticlockwise direction. At Oxford Square, Mr Wiggins would await each car with his camera, and the passengers would be duly photographed, prints being available for purchase later. Many thousands of these cards were produced, and hundreds still survive today in family albums. This example, dated about 1927, is from my family album. It shows my father Ronald wearing his school cap at the rear of the car, holding the guard rail. Standing behind him are his Auntie Sarah and Uncle Joe.

2. The toastrack cars were a familiar sight on the Promenade from 1911 until the first years of the Second World War. Seen in 1912, car 76 turns off the Promenade into Station Road, with Victoria Pier in the background. It will then return to Talbot Square on the inland route via Royal Oak and Marton. Compare this scene with the later view shown in photograph 41. (Commercial postcard)

3. This photograph very much encapsulates the seafront tramway scene immediately before the introduction of the streamlined cars. Taken in 1931, it shows Promenade trams at Gynn Square, looking south. This point was then a key part of the tramway system. Before 1924, it was where the Promenade track terminated, and met the route of the Fleetwood tramroad, where it emerged onto the promenade from Dickson Road. A new track layout, in use from 1924, connected both parts enabling the Promenade cars to be extended towards Bispham from 1926. The blue Lytham cars were also allowed to run as far as here from the south. In this view, a former Fleetwood company 'Yankee' car 121, built in 1899 and so-called because of its American built truck and electrical equipment, is bound for Fleetwood on the service from the Pleasure Beach. Note the simple 'F' destination denoting Fleetwood. These partly open sided combination cars were rebuilt and enclosed by the Corporation being referred to thereafter for obvious reasons, as 'Glasshouses'. Two Dreadnought cars of similar vintage can also be seen, car 60 on the left is loading for the promenade using the unique front loading steps, whilst the right hand example is bound for Bispham. Between these is 1924 built Lytham 'Pullman' car 45, about to reverse to return to its home ground, a journey of 12 miles/19km. The 'Pullman' designation referred to the sumptuous leather seating in the lower deck. All these cars had disappeared by 1935, except the Lytham car which survived until the end of that system in 1937.

4. Blackpool's town routes, to Layton, Central Drive, Lytham Road and Marton were largely in the hands of the 42 'Standard' cars built between 1922 and 1929. These were 78 seat bogie cars with open balconies. Seven cars were built by Hurst Nelson, the remainder by the Corporation in its own workshops. From 1930 onwards they received drivers' vestibules and in addition seventeen were fitted with totally enclosed top decks. Withdrawals began in the 1940s and after 1952, when these cars were ousted from Marton duties by railcars, only nine remained, including car 40, the sole remaining open balcony example. The final four Standards (147, 158 159, 160) lasted until the end of the 1966 season. Red liveried car 48 is seen at Lytham Road terminus in 1933. Built in 1928 with a top cover from an earlier car, it had been vestibuled in 1931 and fully enclosed in 1938. It ran until withdrawal in October 1962, being the last car from Royal Oak to Marton on 28th of that month. Subsequently, it was shipped to America and is now an exhibit in a transport museum in Portland, Oregon. (R.Elliott/ Travel Lens Photographic)

5. The final design of cars introduced to Blackpool before the streamliners was a batch of ten 'Pullman' single deckers delivered in 1928. They were used exclusively on the North Station to Fleetwood service throughout their whole lives. Built by English Electric, these stylish cars had fully cushioned seating and a prominent clerestory roof. These cars were the first to have a trolley tower, to which a pantograph was attached, resulting in them forever being known as the 'Pantographs', even though conventional trolleys were used after 1933. The influx of streamlined cars resulted in the 'Pantograph' cars being used only in the summer months after 1935 until the outbreak of war. From 1952, they again reverted to seasonal use only, and the last occasion that this type operated in service was at Easter 1961. They were always used on the number 1 North Station service. The first of the batch, car 167, is seen at Fleetwood terminus in August 1933, in the newly introduced green livery, and with a pantograph, soon to be replaced with a conventional trolley. From 1954 this car was used as an engineering car, and because of this survived to be preserved at the National Tramway Museum at Crich, being restored to passenger service condition. It returned to Blackpool in 1985 and again in 1998 for tramway centenary celebrations. (R.Elliott/Travel Lens Photographic)

English Electric Streamliners

➔ 6. The impact of the 84 English Electric streamlined cars that entered service between 1933 and 1935 is reflected in the issue of this commercial postcard, the four prototypes using the manufacturer official views. Clockwise from the top left is railcoach 200 as originally fitted with a pantograph, open top double decker 226, open boat car 225 and covered top double decker 250. More details of these cars are given in the remaining captions in this section. (Geoff Smith coll.)

7. The prototype railcoach, 200, is seen in this publicity photograph, demonstrating the sliding roof in the open position. Both saloons seated 24 passengers, and it was luxuriously appointed, including clocks, and underfloor tubular heating, a feature that proved troublesome and was eventually removed. Four tip-up seats were provided on the platform. These were not a success as they restricted movement in this area. The car appeared in Blackpool in June 1933, being put on display in the loop at Gynn Square still bearing the pantograph. When it entered public service on the Promenade in late June, it had a normal trolley pole as seen here. Until the production cars started to enter service from December 1933, it was the sole streamliner in use. This view shows details of the four track layout at the Pleasure Beach, with a Fleetwood Box car visible on the right. In 1937, a two track turning loop came into use as described later.

8. The initial production run of 24 railcars, numbered 201 to 224, entered service from December 1933 until the whole batch was on the road by March 1934. They differed from the prototype in being two feet longer in length, to allow slightly more room in the saloons and driving cabs. The dome over the cabs was also shallower. A repeat order for a further 20 railcars, substantially similar to the initial batch was delivered between June and September 1935. These were numbered 264 to 283. In this view, railcoach 206 is seen at the Clifton Drive terminus on the Promenade soon after entering service. Note the 'via Promenade' notice in the saloon window and the small 'house number' chromium fleet number over the centre entrance. This car ran for over 26 years, and was scrapped in September 1961 following accident damage, being the first of the Blackpool streamline cars to be disposed of. (R.Elliott/Travel Lens Photographic)

9. The first double deck streamliners to appear were the open toppers, designated as 'improved dreadnoughts'. The prototype entered service in February 1934 and was numbered 226. The design seated 94 passengers, including 54 wooden seats on the upper deck. In August 1934, the car was renumbered 237 (700) to allow the boat cars to be numbered in logical sequence. The 12-strong production batch delivered in September and October 1934 became cars 238 to 249. The prototype featured a glass windshield at each end of the upper deck (see photograph 6), but this was very soon removed and did not appear on the production batch. It also had a slightly different livery style, with the central cream stripe being lower than on the subsequent cars. All 13 of these cars were rebuilt with top-covers to the general pattern of the covered top streamliners in 1941-2, though they were not given sliding roofs and so they did not have a trolley arch. This is car 242 (705) in service on the Promenade at Gynn Square in mid-1935. Of the 27 streamlined double deckers, this car is the only one that no longer exists, being scrapped after a collision in 1980 at the Pleasure Beach with car 243 (706), which survived, being uniquely converted back to open top form. It runs today named 'Princess Alice'. (Geoff Smith coll.)

10. The 14 covered top double deck streamliners, numbered 250 to 263, began to appear in December 1934, and were all delivered by the following April. They seated 84 passengers, ten less than their open top counterparts, although after the war they were upgraded to 94 seats by the provision of bench seats at each end of the upper deck. Sliding roofs were fitted, resulting in the trolley base being mounted on a shallow arch. The massive appearance of these cars is demonstrated by this mid-1930s photograph of car 252 (715), having its trolley turned at Gynn Square. Note the Lytham open topped car on the left.

11. The 12 open 'boat' cars, officially 'improved toastracks' and numbered 225 to 236, all entered service in 1934. The prototype, 225 (600), which had lower body sides than the others, arrived in February. The rest were delivered in July and August. Unlike the other streamliners, these cars did not result immediately in the demise of the cars they were meant to replace, all the older toastracks running until the early years of the war. Being built for seasonal use, these cars run only in the summer months and on warm autumn days. Four cars (229, 231, 232, 234) were withdrawn and scrapped in 1968 and a further three (226, 228, 606 – formally 235) are now in America. Five survivors remain in Blackpool. Seen here on the North Promenade in pristine condition in April 1949 is 235 (606), which was exported to the Trolleyville Museum in Cleveland Ohio as late as 2000 in exchange for standard car 147 which had proved too tall for operation there. (J.H.Meredith)

LAYTON AND CENTRAL DRIVE

12. In the mid-1930s, the three tram routes which ran on street tracks and that did not involve any Promenade services were not to enjoy the benefit of streamlined cars. The short Layton and Central Drive routes involved single track working close to the town centre, and both were converted to motor bus operation at the end of the 1936 season, the last trams running on 19th October. The Layton trams started at the north side of Talbot Square, running up Talbot Road to terminate at Layton Square a distance of just over a mile. This early 1930s image of Yates's Wine Lodge, a long established and continuing Blackpool landmark dominating Talbot Square, shows, on the left an open balcony Standard car in Talbot Road approaching the terminus of the Layton service. On the extreme right is Clifton Street, used by the Marton trams, one of which, an enclosed Standard, can be seen at the very top of the street. The Marton service was not affected directly by these route closures at this time, and after the war its prospects as a modern tram route improved greatly as will be described later. (Commercial postcard)

➔ 13. Layton terminus, seen here in 1933, was outside the cemetery. Open balcony Standard 146 waits before returning to Talbot Square. The car was new in 1924, vestibuled in 1932 and ran until 1950. (R.Elliott/Travel Lens Photographic)

➘ 14. The Central Drive route started at Hounds Hill, situated almost behind the Tower, beside Feldman's Theatre and near to Central Station. It operated along the length of Central Drive, to the junction with Waterloo Road. Here there was a triangular junction and Central Drive trams either turned left to run to Talbot Square via Marton, or turned right to run via Royal Oak and Station Road to the Promenade at South Pier and open-air baths. Only the track in Central Drive itself was abandoned because the Marton route cars maintained the link from Royal Oak to South Shore in the summer months. Standard car 35 is seen at the Hounds Hill terminus on a journey to South Pier in August 1935. Note the prominent fleet name on the car side – a feature of these cars at the time. In the foreground is a newly delivered Leyland Tiger 'Gondola' open top bus on the Stanley Park service.
(British Commercial Vehicle Museum)

146

FELDMANS
SWINGIN' ALONG
BOOK EARLY
BLACKPOOL CORPORATION
CENTRAL STATION
FV 8126
YY 500
JERK

15. This late 1920s view shows rebuilt Marton 'Box car' 32 approaching the Hounds Hill terminus on the single track. The Central Station is behind the wall on the left. Five of these 1900 built 4 wheel cars were rebuilt with bogies and lengthened in the early 1920s. This one lasted until May 1937. (H.Nicol/National Tramway Museum)

Brush Railcars

16. In 1937, twenty further streamlined trams entered service. The need for these came about because of the cessation of the Lytham St Annes Corporation Tramways in April of that year. Whilst these had run from Squires Gate through to Gynn Square, either via Lytham Road or via the Promenade and Pleasure Beach, the replacement buses all ran via Lytham Road to Talbot Square. This left a gap in the tram service on the Promenade, as well as the ending of the practice of Blackpool hiring all available blue cars for use during the busiest part of the Illumination season. The new cars were intended to compensate for these losses. These were built by Brush of Loughborough to the general luxurious specification of the previous English Electric railcoaches, although for patent reasons, every detail needed to differ in some way. One important difference was that the passenger doors were air operated. They were even dubbed 'railcars' rather than 'railcoaches'. These were the first and only trams of this type built by Brush and they were attractive vehicles with a pronounced taper to the car ends. Mounted on EMB trucks and numbered 284 to 303, the cars entered service during the second half of 1937, initially on a Lytham Road to Fleetwood service. The first car, 284 (621), is seen in this view at the Brush works before delivery to Blackpool. The first ten cars had this paint scheme, whilst the remainder entered service with an attractive green 'V' at each end, a feature which was adopted as standard for the single deck streamline fleet after the war.

SQUIRES GATE AND LYTHAM ROAD

17. Although Blackpool's Lytham Road tram service terminated at the junction with Squires Gate Lane, there was a connecting line from here along Squires Gate Lane to the Promenade tramway at Starr Gate. This was part of the Lytham St Annes system, and indeed their depot was on the south side of Squires Gate Lane. From 1932, this link was used in the eastbound direction by Blackpool's circular tour cars, and this continued until the outbreak of war. During the war, the tracks and overhead remained, although unused. This included the access to the Lytham depot in case emergency storage was required for Blackpool's fleet. In 1957, it was decided to resurrect the circular tour service, and the partially tarred over tracks were uncovered and brought back into use, cars running from the Promenade to Lytham Road as before. This section was always included in the itinerary of enthusiasts' tours as shown here. On 22nd June 1958 standard car 41 is seen in Starr Gate, opposite the promenade tram terminus. It is negotiating the former triangular junction used by Lytham cars to and from Clifton Drive towards St Annes. The junction with the Promenade track is in the right distance (see photograph 46). (C.W.Routh)

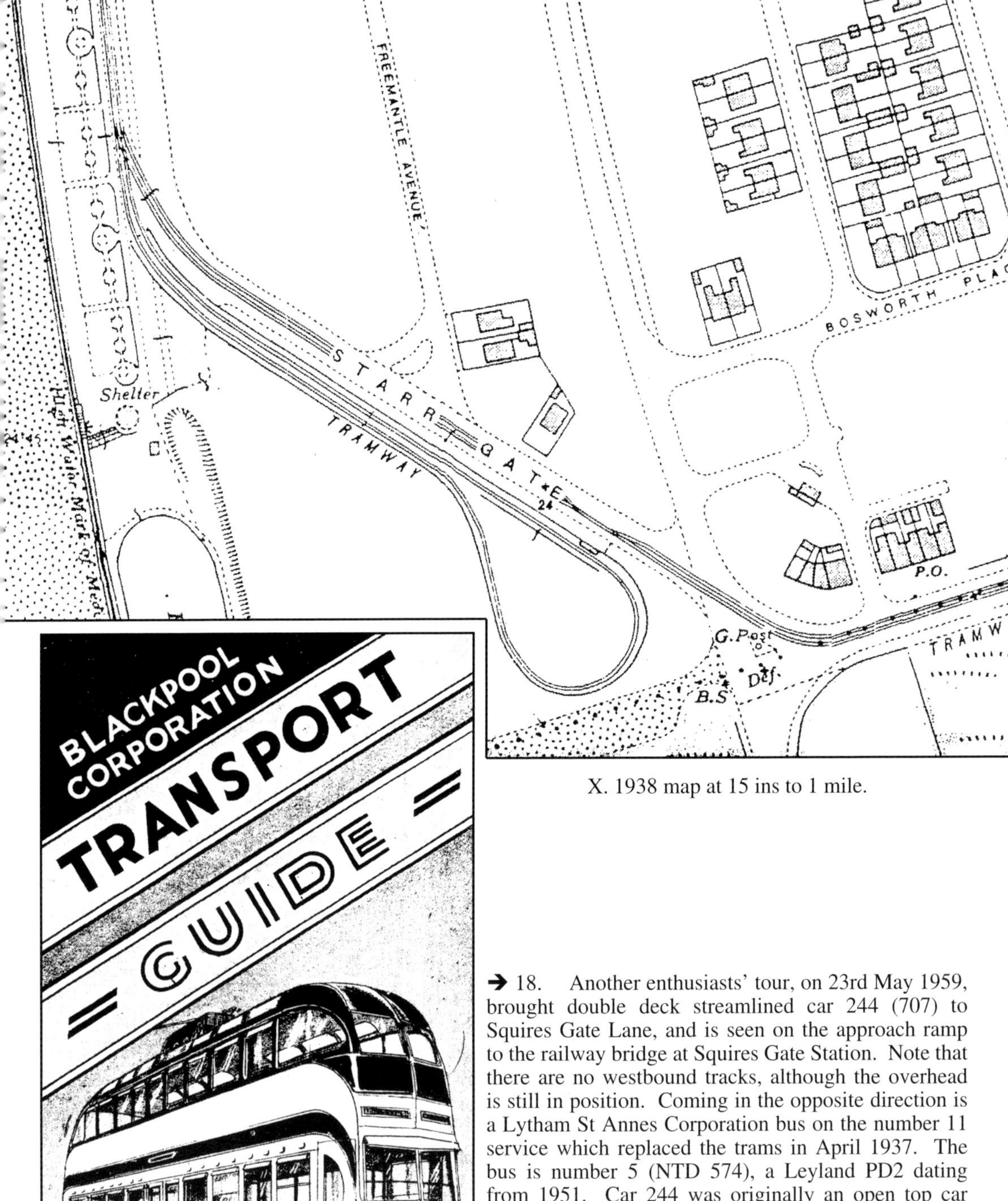

X. 1938 map at 15 ins to 1 mile.

➔ 18. Another enthusiasts' tour, on 23rd May 1959, brought double deck streamlined car 244 (707) to Squires Gate Lane, and is seen on the approach ramp to the railway bridge at Squires Gate Station. Note that there are no westbound tracks, although the overhead is still in position. Coming in the opposite direction is a Lytham St Annes Corporation bus on the number 11 service which replaced the trams in April 1937. The bus is number 5 (NTD 574), a Leyland PD2 dating from 1951. Car 244 was originally an open top car and given a top cover in 1941/2. The upper deck front windows are shallower with a greater back slope than the original covered top streamliners, and there is no trolley arch. Squires Gate Station, on the coastal line between Blackpool Central and Kirkham, is still open, but is a single platform unmanned halt on the single track line which now terminates at Blackpool South. (C.W.Routh)

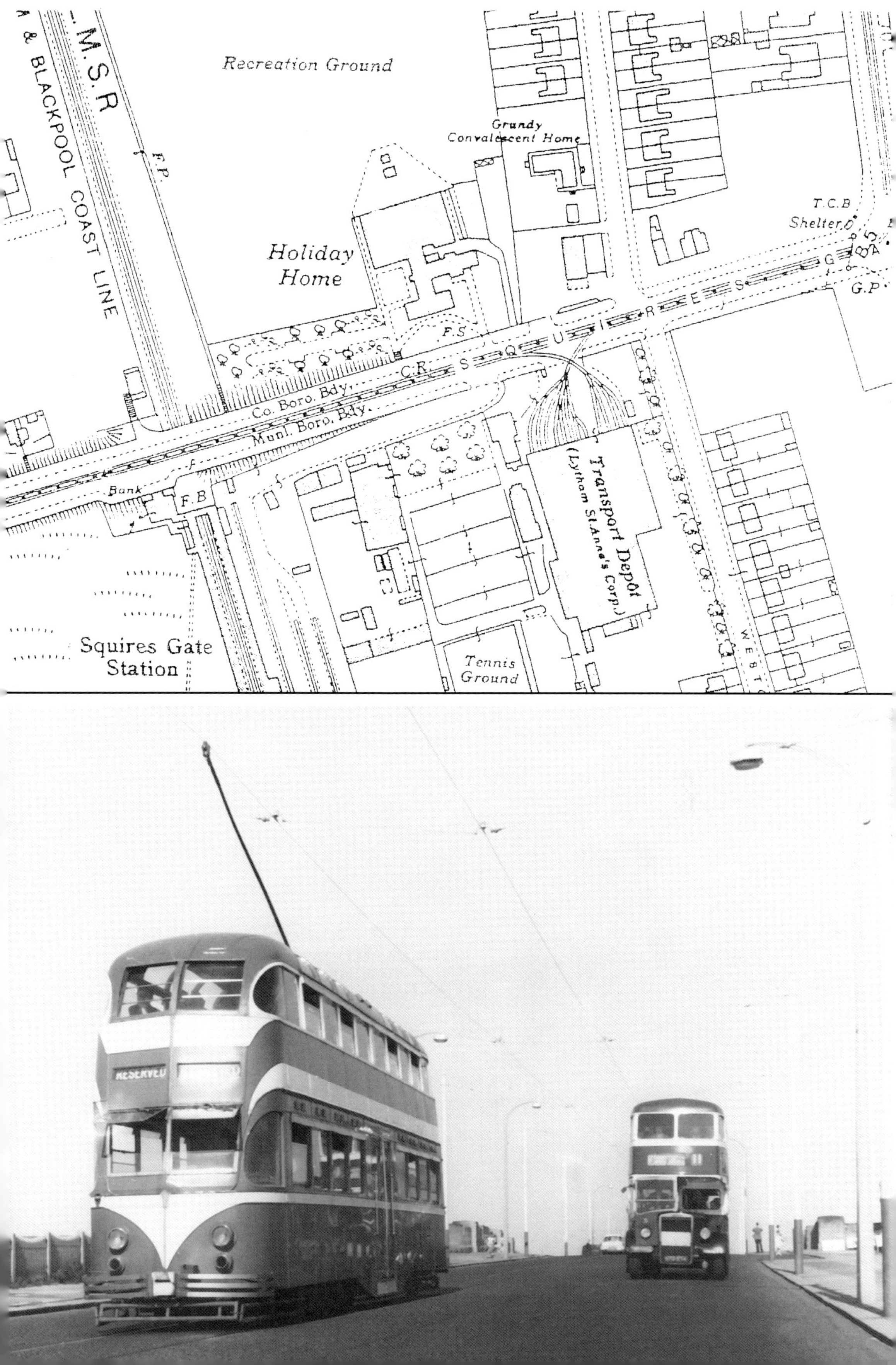
L.M.S.R
& BLACKPOOL COAST LINE
Recreation Ground
Grundy
Convalescent Home
Holiday
Home
F.P.
F.S
C.R.
Co. Boro. Bdy.
Munl. Boro. Bdy.
S Q U I R E S G A
T.C.B
Shelter
G.P
B 5
Bank
F.B
Transport Depot
(Lytham St.Anne's Corp.)
Tennis
Ground
Squires Gate
Station
RESERVED

19. Opposite the end of Lytham Road, at the other side of the railway bridge is the entrance to Blackpool Airport. This pre-war view shows a circular tour boat car about to turn into Lytham Road. On the right is the Greyhound Stadium which disappeared with the development of the air facilities during the war. The car is the prototype boat 225 (600), which has shallower sides than the production batch. On 27th June 2008, this car was named *Duchess of Cornwall* as mentioned earlier in the book

→ 20. This is Lytham Road terminus, showing its proximity to Blackpool Airport. On 23rd June 1958, a Brush railcar waits as standard 41 on private tour duty turns from Squires Gate Lane, having used the link tracks from Starr Gate. From 1958, the Brush cars from Bispham depot operated the seven car service from here to Bispham, alternating with the six car service to Cabin normally operated with streamlined double deckers. (D.F.Parker)

→ 21. Looking along Lytham Road from the terminus, a streamlined double decker approaches the terminus in June 1954. As can be seen, Lytham Road ran as straight as a die for most of the way into the town centre. Blackpool Tower is in the distance. (R.J.S.Wiseman)

BLACKPOOL AIRPORT
BISPHAM
BISPHAM

LITTLE BISPHAM

22. This is a typical Blackpool street scene from the 1950s. Double decker car 240 (703) has just passed the junction with Watson Road on its way to Squires Gate, whilst Standard car 41, still touring, is preceded by a police sergeant and a constable on bicycles. The 1950s cars complete the scene, dated 23rd June 1958. (D.F.Parker)

23. A Squires Gate bound double decker climbs the slope over the Skew Bridge where the coastal railway running into Central Station passed under Lytham Road. A railcoach is proceeding in the opposite direction towards the Promenade. Just beyond the bridge is the junction with Station Road, where, as can be seen here, some Marton cars turned off to run down to South Pier (see photographs 39 and 40). In earlier times, there was a triangular junction here, enabling Lytham trams to run from the Squires Gate direction to South Shore. In the right background can be seen the extensive railway provision around Blackpool South Station. Situated here was the junction of the coastal line with the direct line from Kirkham. Today, the only rail presence is the single track of the coastal branch which terminates at Blackpool South, and most of the area is devoted to car parking.

XII. 1938 map at 15 ins to 1 mile.

DOG & PARTRIDGE HOTEL
DOG & PARTRIDGE HOTEL
DOG & PARTRIDGE HOTEL
RESERVED
LFR 646
CAFE

← 24. At the Waterloo Road junction was a triangular track layout beside the Royal Oak, terminus of the Marton tram route. The Lytham Road cars passed straight through, and as previously mentioned, some Marton cars turned into Lytham Road to travel to South Shore via Station Road. The tracks allowing access to Waterloo Road from the Promenade direction, and vice-versa were rarely used, but on 13th June 1954, boat car 229 turns left from Lytham Road into Waterloo Road during an enthusiasts' tour. This car was one of those scrapped in 1968. The Dog and Partridge pub, visible on the corner of Waterloo Road has since relocated 'next door', slightly further along Lytham Road on the site of the coach park which can just be seen in this view. (R.J.S.Wiseman)

← 25. At its northern end, Lytham Road turns west to join the Promenade at Manchester Square. At Hopton Road, the tracks connecting with the depot at Rigby Road joined the Lytham Road route. In the early 1950s, a railcar is seen here having just negotiated the track junction at Hopton Road, on a service to Cabin. (J.Fozard)

26. This double decker is at the end of Lytham Road and is about to cross the road and rumble onto the Promenade tracks. The car has yet to receive the modernised single destination layout as seen on car 240 in photograph 22. A programme to convert all the double deck streamliners was commenced in 1955 with car 250 (713), and this proved to be quite prolonged, the process only being completed in 1980. The art deco frontage of the Manchester Hotel, built in 1936, can just be seen to the right of the tram. This famous Blackpool venue was demolished in the 1990s and replaced with a new building. (J.Fozard)

Sun Saloons and Vambacs

27. The final English Electric streamlined trams built were these 12 cars delivered to Blackpool in August 1939, just before the start of war and numbered 10 to 21 in the fleet. They were cheaply constructed semi-open cars, meant to replace the Fleetwood 'racks'. The motors and control equipment were salvaged from scrapped cars and the bodies could be described as boat cars with semi-covered tops. Thus they had wooden seating, no drivers partition and waist high passenger doors. The glazing was half height and the roofs had roller shutter covers. Known as 'Sun Saloons', and obviously meant for summer use only, visually these cars were very striking with streamlined tapered fronts more exaggerated than even the Brush railcars. Unpopular with passengers because of the draughty ride they gave, the cars were fully enclosed in the early part of the war and used to transport troops daily to the rifle range at Rossall, where a special loop was constructed (see photograph 108). Immediately after the war they reverted to Promenade duties. From 1948 to 1952 they were upgraded with cushioned seats, Maley and Taunton resilient trucks and Vambac control equipment for operation on the newly relaid tracks of the Marton route. Sun Saloon car 18 is seen in this mid 1940s view working on the Promenade at the Pleasure Beach. The car is fully enclosed but still with wooden seats and it does not appear to have yet been fitted with drivers cab partitions. Note that on the lower side of the car, near the front corner, the word 'Blackpool' has been blacked out from the Transport Departments title – a wartime measure designed to confuse the enemy. (W.J.Haynes)

28. Blackpool was in the forefront in testing the latest tramway technology. In the years after the war, two cars were experimentally fitted with Maley and Taunton resilient silent running trucks and Vambac control equipment. These cars were railcoach 208 and Brush railcar 303. After protracted trials, it was decided to fit the Sun Saloon cars, then being transferred to the Marton route, with this equipment. This was fitted between 1949 and 1952, the cars then being known as 'Marton Vambacs'. Experimental railcoach 208 was also put to work at Marton, but the Brush railcar 303, because of its unsuitable power doors, remained with the rest of the Brush cars working from Bispham depot. Being a one-off car, it was unpopular and rarely used (see photograph 92). Vambac fitted railcoach 208 is seen in this view at Fleetwood Ferry terminus operating an enthusiasts' tour shortly before being transferred to Marton depot. Note the Maley and Taunton inside framed trucks and the unique windscreens fitted to this car. An orthodox Brush railcar on the North Station service is standing alongside. (J.H.Meredith)

VAMBAC

The Vambac system of tramcar control was a post war innovation, marketed under licence from the USA by Crompton Parkinson Ltd of Chelmsford. The name is an acronym of the system's description: Variable Automatic Multinotch Braking and Acceleration Control. It was Britain's version of the control gear fitted to the famous Electric Railway Presidents' Conference Committee (PCC) design of streetcar developed in the 1930s. The normal tram controller was dispensed with, and instead, the driver had a single lever mounted to the left of the seat. Pushing this forward gave acceleration, and pushing it backwards gave braking down to 4mph, with the conventional air brake producing the final stop. A drum, housed above the centre entrance well and below the trolley tower, contained the circular bank of multinotches, which controlled the extremely smooth motion of the car. The Vambac system came too late to affect tramway development, which had all but ceased in Britain. In addition to the 39 Blackpool cars which eventually had this equipment, the only applications elsewhere were on experimental cars – a single ended double deck car in Glasgow (car 1005 – built 1947) and a single deck railcar in Leeds (car 602 - built 1953). This latter car is now preserved at the National Tramway Museum at Crich and retains its Vambac equipment, as does privately owned Blackpool Coronation car 304, which runs occasionally at Blackpool in the summer season, demonstrating the superb riding characteristics of these cars.

MARTON AND ROYAL OAK

29. Blackpool's only remaining all street route surviving after 1936 was to Marton and Royal Oak. The track was relaid after the war, and railcoaches introduced as described earlier, although until 1952, some older Standard double deck cars were still required to run on the route. This view, dated 22 June 1952, demonstrates the mixed Sun Saloon and Standard operation, showing Standard 100 setting off from the Talbot Square terminus of the service, and starting to climb Clifton Street. In the distance, on the terminal stub, a former Sun Saloon is having its trolley turned. On the extreme right is the side of Yates Wine Lodge – note the sign over the doorway 'Champagne on Draught'. (R.J.S.Wiseman)

MARKET
ABINGDON STREET
MARTON
RESTAURANT

← 30. This is a close up view of Marton Vambac car 16 at the Talbot Square terminus. Two tracks were available. The left hand track led onto the Promenade tracks via a trailing connection, this being used by the boat cars on the circular tour, which loaded here. Note the 'Bundy' time clock beside the car, used by guards who had to 'clock in' before the car departed. (D.F.Parker)

← 31. The Marton Route ran through some of the town's shopping streets. From Clifton Street, there was a sharp right turn into Abingdon Street, followed by a left turn into Church Street. This busy scene outside the Market in Abingdon Street shows open balcony Standard car 40 on tour, using the crossover at the top of Birley Street. Also in view is a Brush railcar, a type not normally seen here, whilst a Marton Vambac car in normal service waits patiently to proceed from Church Street towards Talbot Square. In the background is the Opera House, part of the Winter Gardens entertainment complex. (C.W.Routh)

32. Seen in Church Street, looking towards Devonshire Square, this Marton Vambac is waiting at the Cookson Street traffic lights. The Regal cinema, showing 'Seven Brides for Seven Brothers', can be seen on the extreme right. In the distance is another of Blackpool's distinctive art deco buildings, the Raikes Garage, built in 1938 which now houses a solicitor's business. The Vambac equipment was mounted at the base of the trolley tower in the enclosed compartment visible in this view of the tram. (J.Fozard)

33. After passing through Devonshire Square, the Marton trams turned south along the tree lined Whitegate Drive. Here, at the Knowsley Avenue junction, is one of the railcoaches transferred to the route after 1952 to replace the remaining standard double deck cars. The proximity to Stanley Park, only a short distance to the east, is indicated by the signpost on the corner. Note the lack of traffic; today this junction is one of many on Whitegate Drive controlled by traffic lights. (J.Fozard)

➔ 34. This is Whitegate Drive where it curves near Beechfield Avenue looking towards Devonshire Square. Note the 'Tram Pinch' road sign on the left, warning motorists that the distance between the kerb and the track was about to reduce. This sign, common in the days of traditional street tramways, does not appear in the present day Highway Code and would baffle today's drivers. Standard car 49, on enthusiasts' tour duty in 1961, is re-living its days on the Marton route. It is now preserved at the National Tramway Museum at Crich. (C.W.Routh)

➔ 35. Marton tram depot was situated at the south end of Whitegate Drive, near the Saddle Inn. This dated from 1901 and housed the cars used on the town routes. It had capacity for 40 cars on 8 roads. Following the closure of the Layton and Central Drive services in 1936, the spare capacity at the depot was filled by housing the boat cars here. The depot was closed to trams during the war, and the premises used for aircraft parts production. Seen pausing on the three track layout in front of the depot on 17th April 1949 is upgraded Sun Saloon car 12. The vacant space at the foot of the trolley tower indicates that it has yet to receive Vambac control equipment, and it would be almost a further three years before it did so. The number series of these cars, was completely out of sequence with the earlier streamlined cars. This raises the question whether these were the first cars to use a planned reconfiguration of the numbering of the whole fleet, possibly frustrated by the outbreak of war, when more important matters would prevail. (J.H.Meredith)

DEPOT
TRAM
PINCH
49

36. Looking towards Oxford Square in 1957, the three track layout in front of the depot is in full use here, with Vambac cars on the running lines and Standard car 40 on the depot access track. Note the passenger shelter in the depot entrance. The Vambac cars are displaying the change occurring at this time from the more flamboyant, yet very attractive paint scheme including the green 'V' on the car dash panels, to a more plain livery. (C.W.Routh)

➔ 37. Shortly after passing the depot, the route turned west at Oxford Square into Waterloo Road. This is the scene near Oxford Square showing a car in Waterloo Road proceeding towards Royal Oak. The building with the decorated gable end in the background is on the corner of Kirkstall Avenue. The Corporation bus, no 288 (EFV 288), is one of the 100 streamlined centre entrance Leyland PD2 models delivered after the war. (C.Barker coll.)

➔ 38. The Royal Oak terminus of the Marton route was at the junction with Waterloo Road and Lytham Road, where there was a triangular track junction with the Lytham Road route. Most Marton cars terminated here, and the busy nature of the junction meant that a trolley reverser was provided, which can be seen to the right of the Vambac car. On the left is Standard car 40 on tour, standing outside the Palladium Cinema. The trams approached the terminus by crossing the railway bridge at Blackpool South station, the entrance of which can be seen in the right background of this 1958 view. (D.F.Parker)

MARTON
RESERVED

RESERVED
CINEMA
TALBOT
MARTON
POOL SOUTH

STATION ROAD AND SOUTH SHORE

39. As noted earlier, during the summer months some Marton route journeys were extended to Station Road, South Shore. These trams turned left at the Waterloo Road junction and ran along Lytham Road to turn right into Station Road, terminating opposite the Promenade and the South Pier (see photograph 24). This view shows a Vambac car in Station Road returning from South Shore to Talbot Square via Marton. (J.Fozard)

➔ 40. This is a scene dating from 1957 at the South Shore terminus, looking towards the Promenade with a Vambac car ready to depart. When Standard cars operated this service, they displayed 'South Pier and Baths', denoting the proximity to the open-air baths which were adjacent to the Pier. Note the single track connection from the southbound Promenade track on the right. The variety performers appearing at the Pier in 1957 included Denny Willis and 'Wilson, Keppel and Betty', who were performing their famous sand dance act. (J.Fozard)

Coronations and Twin Cars

41. Rolling stock developments in the 1950s concentrated on provision for the Promenade service. In accordance with the policy at the time, 25 high speed, high capacity, single deck cars, entered service between 1952 and 1954. These were the 'Coronation' cars, built by Charles Roberts of Wakefield. They were 50 feet long and almost 8 feet wide, six feet longer and five inches wider than the railcoaches, seating 56 passengers. Using the Vambac control technology with Maley and Taunton silent running trucks, these cars were intended to provide the year round service on the core seafront tramway to Fleetwood. Numbered 304 to 328, the first car, 304, was delivered in June 1952 and was launched into service at a ceremony on the 16th of that month. Deliveries continued through 1952 and 1953 until the final car, 328, entered service in early 1954. Their striking modern lines, even by today's standards, are evident in this view of newly delivered car 321 (658) standing on the centre track at Bispham in June 1953. Note the decorative plaques, commemorating the Queen's Coronation, fitted to the trolley tower above the Vambac housing. These smooth and fast cars, with all round glazing in the saloons, were an immediate hit with the public. (R.F.Mack)

42. By the mid-1950s, the policy favouring single deckers had changed, and maximum capacity was then seen as paramount. This favoured the double deck cars, even though they needed two guards. Consideration was also given to increasing the capacity of the single deckers, resulting in an experiment to create a continental style tram / trailer set. This would operate using the powered tram on its own in slack times, and coupled with the trailer to give much greater carrying capacity at the busiest times. In 1957, railcoaches 276 (676) and 275 (675) were rebuilt into this tram / trailer combination, fully modernised with front ends resembling the Coronation cars. 275 was stripped of its motors and controllers to become the trailer car. In a striking livery of all over white, the set was officially launched into service on 9th April 1958. Union objections to their use meant that initially the set could only be used on a 'Coastal Tour', which ran three times daily from Central Station, to Fleetwood, Starr Gate and return. From 1959, a further eight railcoaches, nos 272 to 274 and 277 to 281, were rebuilt into towing cars, and ten new trailers (T1 to T10), seating 66 passengers were built by Metropolitan Cammell. Car 275 was converted back to a powered car in early 1961. The resultant ten 'Twin Car' sets then operated a limited stop service on the Promenade, turning at the loops on the system. The original tram / trailer set is seen here at Central Station on 22nd June 1958, loading before departing on the Coastal Tour. Trailer car 275 is nearest the camera.
(D.Tate)

➔ 43. The southern terminus of the Promenade route was near the junction of Clifton Drive and Squires Gate Lane. The tramway had been extended along the New South Promenade from the Pleasure Beach in late 1926, regular services commencing the following year. The original terminus was near Abercorn Place, and beyond the crossover there was a lengthy double track stub, anticipating a further extension of the Promenade towards St Annes that in the event never took place. In 1934, the prototype open top streamliner, in its unique livery, is seen at the terminus, before moving up to reverse at the crossover. It is running with its original fleet number 226 and before the rest of the batch was delivered. During this period it operated on the South Promenade to Bispham service alongside the new railcoaches and with the top deck closed. From August 1934, this car was numbered 237 (700).
(R.Elliott/Travel Lens Photographic)

STARR GATE AND SOUTH PROMENADE

44. In 1938, the South Promenade tramway was extended from its temporary terminus to run alongside Clifton Drive nearer to Squires Gate Lane. Here a large turning circle was constructed and the terminus was known as Starr Gate, although trams routinely continued to show 'South Promenade' until the 1960s. During the war a siding was installed just before the terminus shelter, but this was short lived, being removed by 1950. In this 1950s view, a railcoach stands at the terminus, with a boat car and a double decker waiting behind. The curved track of the circle has been renewed in May 2008. (J.Fozard)

45. This car, having left the terminus, has just negotiated the turning circle amongst the sand dunes and is facing north on a journey to Fleetwood, almost twelve miles away. This is a comparatively rare view of towing car 281 (671) running without its trailer which was normally trailer T1 (681). Although the 'Twin Car' sets were designed to be split in less busy periods, it was not often that the towing cars ran on their own. (D.F.Parker)

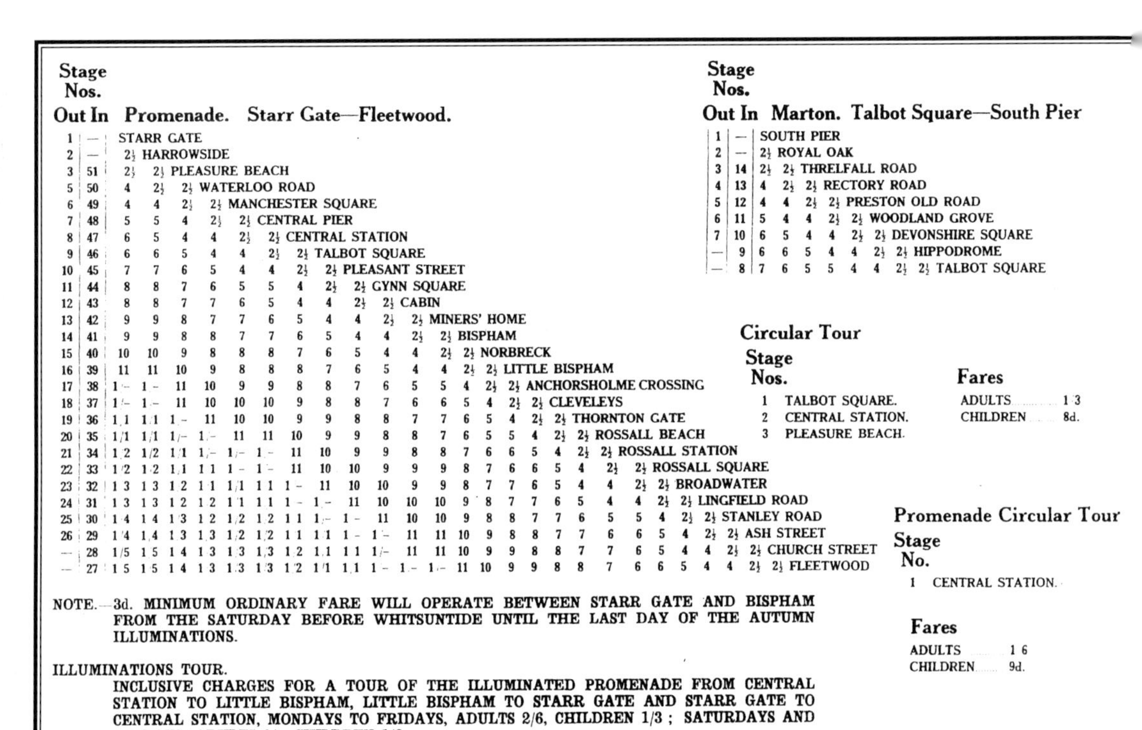

Promenade. Starr Gate—Fleetwood.

Stage Nos. Out	In	Fares	Stage
1	—		STARR GATE
2	—	2½	HARROWSIDE
3	51	2½ 2½	PLEASURE BEACH
5	50	4 2½ 2½	WATERLOO ROAD
6	49	4 4 2½ 2½	MANCHESTER SQUARE
7	48	5 5 4 2½ 2½	CENTRAL PIER
8	47	6 5 4 4 2½ 2½	CENTRAL STATION
9	46	6 6 5 4 4 2½ 2½	TALBOT SQUARE
10	45	7 7 6 5 4 4 2½ 2½	PLEASANT STREET
11	44	8 8 7 6 5 5 4 2½ 2½	GYNN SQUARE
12	43	8 8 7 7 6 5 4 4 2½ 2½	CABIN
13	42	9 9 8 7 7 6 5 4 4 2½ 2½	MINERS' HOME
14	41	9 9 8 8 7 7 6 5 4 4 2½ 2½	BISPHAM
15	40	10 10 9 8 8 8 7 6 5 4 4 2½ 2½	NORBRECK
16	39	11 11 10 9 8 8 8 7 6 5 4 4 2½ 2½	LITTLE BISPHAM
17	38	1/- 1/- 11 10 9 9 8 8 7 6 5 5 4 2½ 2½	ANCHORSHOLME CROSSING
18	37	1/- 1/- 11 10 10 10 9 8 8 7 6 6 5 4 2½ 2½	CLEVELEYS
19	36	1/1 1/1 1/- 11 10 10 9 9 8 8 7 7 6 5 4 2½ 2½	THORNTON GATE
20	35	1/1 1/1 1/- 1/- 11 11 10 9 9 8 8 7 6 5 5 4 2½ 2½	ROSSALL BEACH
21	34	1/2 1/2 1/1 1/- 1/- 1/- 11 10 9 9 8 8 7 6 6 5 4 2½ 2½	ROSSALL STATION
22	33	1/2 1/2 1/1 1/1 1/- 1/- 11 10 10 9 9 9 8 7 6 6 5 4 2½ 2½	ROSSALL SQUARE
23	32	1/3 1/3 1/2 1/1 1/1 1/1 1/- 11 10 10 9 9 8 7 7 6 5 4 4 2½ 2½	BROADWATER
24	31	1/3 1/3 1/2 1/2 1/1 1/1 1/- 1/- 11 10 10 10 9 8 7 7 6 5 4 4 2½ 2½	LINGFIELD ROAD
25	30	1/4 1/4 1/3 1/2 1/2 1/2 1/1 1/- 1/- 11 10 10 9 8 8 7 7 6 5 5 4 2½ 2½	STANLEY ROAD
26	29	1/4 1/4 1/3 1/3 1/2 1/2 1/1 1/1 1/- 1/- 11 11 10 9 8 8 7 7 6 6 5 4 2½ 2½	ASH STREET
—	28	1/5 1/5 1/4 1/3 1/3 1/3 1/2 1/1 1/1 1/- 11 11 10 9 9 8 8 7 7 6 5 4 4 2½ 2½	CHURCH STREET
—	27	1/5 1/5 1/4 1/3 1/3 1/3 1/2 1/1 1/1 1/- 1/- 1/- 11 10 9 9 8 8 7 6 6 5 4 4 2½ 2½	FLEETWOOD

NOTE.—3d. MINIMUM ORDINARY FARE WILL OPERATE BETWEEN STARR GATE AND BISPHAM FROM THE SATURDAY BEFORE WHITSUNTIDE UNTIL THE LAST DAY OF THE AUTUMN ILLUMINATIONS.

ILLUMINATIONS TOUR.
INCLUSIVE CHARGES FOR A TOUR OF THE ILLUMINATED PROMENADE FROM CENTRAL STATION TO LITTLE BISPHAM, LITTLE BISPHAM TO STARR GATE AND STARR GATE TO CENTRAL STATION, MONDAYS TO FRIDAYS, ADULTS 2/6, CHILDREN 1/3 ; SATURDAYS AND SUNDAYS, ADULTS 3/-, CHILDREN 1/6.

Marton. Talbot Square—South Pier

Stage Nos. Out	In	Fares	Stage
1	—		SOUTH PIER
2	—	2½	ROYAL OAK
3	14	2½ 2½	THRELFALL ROAD
4	13	4 2½ 2½	RECTORY ROAD
5	12	4 4 2½ 2½	PRESTON OLD ROAD
6	11	5 4 4 2½ 2½	WOODLAND GROVE
7	10	6 5 4 4 2½ 2½	DEVONSHIRE SQUARE
—	9	6 6 5 4 4 2½ 2½	HIPPODROME
—	8	7 6 5 5 4 4 2½ 2½	TALBOT SQUARE

Circular Tour

Stage Nos.	
1	TALBOT SQUARE.
2	CENTRAL STATION.
3	PLEASURE BEACH.

Fares

ADULTS	1/3
CHILDREN	8d.

Promenade Circular Tour

Stage No.	
1	CENTRAL STATION.

Fares

ADULTS	1/6
CHILDREN	9d.

46. A Brush railcar, still in the wartime green livery, is about to turn onto the promenade track, near to the pre 1938 terminus after leaving Starr Gate The connection to the Lytham St Annes street track can be seen behind the fence in this view dated April 1949. (J.H.Meredith)

47. This June 1952 scene is taken slightly further north than the previous photograph, and shows two Brush railcars, both in the brighter post war livery. The double track junction with the street tracks leading to Squires Gate Lane and St Annes is clearly seen. These tracks were disused until 1957, when the eastbound one was brought back into use for circular tours. Note that in the three years since the previous photograph, the familiar 'Welcome to Blackpool' arch over the roadway has appeared. (R.J.S.Wiseman)

48. An interesting view of the Lifeboat illuminated feature car, seen at dusk approaching Starr Gate terminus just beyond the junction with the street tracks. This car, formerly Marton Box car 40 and 'launched' in 1926, was in service every Illumination season until 1961 as a mobile exhibit. It was only in 1959 that it was adapted to carry passengers, a move that weakened the already ageing structure and sealed its fate. On the right can be seen one of the illuminated tableaux, a feature of this area during the illuminations.

49. Between Starr Gate and the Pleasure Beach, there is an intermediate crossover at Harrowside. This saw regular use in the 1950s and 1960s, and services ran from here to Cabin and Bispham, and for ten days in May 2008, all South Promenade cars had to reverse here due to the closure of the Starr Gate turning circle for track renewal. Seen turning here on 27th December 1965 is railcoach 224 (610), in the half green and cream livery which was being introduced at this time. By then it was the last first series railcoach in public service, and it was rebuilt in the 1970s to become One Man Operated (OMO) car 3. Note the substantial Promenade shelter on the left, typical of those on the new South Promenade. (L.G.Sidwell)

PLEASURE BEACH AND MANCHESTER SQUARE

50. The Pleasure Beach is one of the world's major pleasure parks and, since the Promenade trams were extended to here in 1903, has always been a major destination for tramway passengers. In the 1930s, there was a four track layout here to accommodate terminating trams. This interesting commercial view shows two railcoaches and a Dreadnought car in its last season of service. The prominent Casino building was replaced in the late 1930s by the famous art deco building that still stands near today's tram terminus. (Geoff Smith coll.)

51. The new turning arrangement at the Pleasure Beach, introduced in 1937, comprised a two track duo-directional flattened circle. In April 1949, railcoach 275, having run around the circle in an anti-clockwise direction, rejoins the main line. There was also a loop off the northbound main tracks inside the circle, which can be seen in front of the car in this view. Car 275 was later rebuilt into the prototype unpowered trailer car, and later still was remotored to pull trailer T5. It still runs today as car 675 towing trailer 685. (J.H.Meredith)

52. Two cars are seen loading within the circle at the Pleasure Beach in the early 1950s. Boat car 232, which was scrapped in 1968, is behind open balcony Standard car 36, withdrawn in 1954. The turning circle here has been significantly altered in 2008, and is now one way (anti-clockwise) with an additional internal loop to provide additional storage space for trams laying over duiring crew meal breaks. (A.D.Packer)

53. In the mid-1960s, some of the illuminated feature cars were used in the daylight summer months on the Promenade 'Circular Tour'. This ran from the Tower to Little Bispham, then through Blackpool to Starr Gate, before returning to the Tower. This view shows the Western Train, a very popular tram / trailer set built in 1962. The 'Locomotive' was constructed from former railcoach 222, and the 'coach' is former 'Pantograph' car 174. It is seen here passing the Pleasure Beach on the last leg of its tour. Out of use since 1999 for safety reasons, this car is today being rebuilt using Lottery grants and is due to re-enter service in 2009. (Commercial postcard)

54. A panorama of the Central Promenade, looking north from South Pier is seen here, showing a Coronation car. In the right foreground, a railcoach waits at the Station Road terminus of the Marton service (see photograph 41). Note the single track connection into Station Road from the Promenade. (Commercial postcard)

TWIN-CAR
STARR GATE
VIA PLEASURE BEACH
275

← 55. On 23rd October 1966, track engineering works were taking place just north of Waterloo Road, where the windmill on the Promenade was a prominent feature. This has recently been removed as part of the Promenade reconstruction works which are still on-going in 2008. Railcoach 267 (614), newly overhauled and repainted including an orange trolley tower, negotiates the section in 1966. In 1973, this car was totally rebuilt, becoming OMO car 10. In the distance is Brush railcar 302 (638), which was later rebuilt into a prototype OMO car, but never operated as such. It was withdrawn in 1980. (L.G.Sidwell)

56. The evening shadows lengthen, as trams pass on the Promenade near to Manchester Square. Trailer car 275 (675) is heading south to Starr Gate on a limited stop service passing a railcoach and Coronation car 313. Car 313 had a short life in passenger service, being withdrawn in 1963 to provide a spare set of trucks for the other Coronations. After languishing some time in Bispham depot, its body was scrapped in 1966. (J.Fozard)

57. The promenade stop at Manchester Square was always very busy. Being the nearest stop to Rigby Road depot, all crew changes occurred here. The proximity to the Coliseum Coach station also meant that this stop was used by trippers arriving by coach. The shelter mounted clock is prominent in this view of double deck car 247 (710) leaving the stop, pursued by Coronation car 311 (648). Car 247, as 710, has achieved fame later in its career on two counts. In 1984 and 1985, the car was loaned to the National Tramway Museum Crich. This is the only occasion to date when one of these double deck streamlined cars has been moved away from Blackpool. In 1989. it 'hit and fatally injured' the TV soap 'Coronation Street' character Alan Bradley at the Pleasant Street stop on North Promenade. The episode showing this was screened on 8th December 1989, but the 'incident' has been regularly repeated on television since then. (J.Fozard)

RIGBY ROAD DEPOT

58. The main tram depot was situated at Rigby Road, reached via a short connecting track from Lytham Road and Hopton Road. This was opened in 1935 as part of the Modernisation Plan and was built specially for the streamlined fleet. Accommodation was provided for 110 cars on 18 roads. Seen on the tracks outside the depot in the early 1950s are two railcoaches, the nearest of which is still in the mainly green livery first applied during the war. The Coliseum coach station can be seen in the background. In the summer all types of coaches could be seen here, including double deck service buses, examples of which are visible on the extreme right of this view. (J.Fozard)

59. A glimpse inside Rigby Road car shed on 22nd June 1952. Brand new Coronation car 304 (641), the first of its type, is seen before being used on its first enthusiasts' tour. The car had been officially launched into service on the Promenade six days earlier. (R.J.S.Wiseman)

FOXHALL, CENTRAL STATION AND THE TOWER

← 60. A railcoach on the Lytham Road to Cabin service picks up passengers at Foxhall Square with Central Pier visible in the background. On the right, another form of Promenade transport is evident. The overhead wiring branching off the Promenade to the right indicates where the single track emergency access link to Rigby Road depot leaves the Promenade to run along Princess Street. This line formally linked to the original 1885 tram depot at Blundell Street. This building was demolished in 1983 and the area is now a car park. However, the site is one of three possibilities for the new depot to house Blackpool's proposed new fleet of 16 super trams. Accordingly, the junction of the Princess Street link with the Promenade track has been upgraded in the large track improvement programme undertaken in the winter of 2007 – 2008, including the provision of new crossovers. (J.Fozard)

← 61. Seen in 1960 near Foxhall Square is double deck car 243 (706). In 1959, six of these cars still retained their green wartime livery and when advertising was introduced onto cars, their livery was modified with a central cream area. The cars involved were 237, 238, 242, 243, 244 and 246. Today, this car is the open top car 'Princess Alice', having been converted back to its original open-top condition for the 1985 Tramway centenary following serious accident damage.

62. At Central Pier, with the 1937-built Lifeboat House in the background, a Coronation car proceeds south on a hot day, judging by the open windscreen. These cars soon lost their frontal decorative chrome strips, and later the fleet number was applied in the vacant space. The following railcoach is showing 'Highfield Road' on its destination screens. There was a crossover at this point which was on the Lytham Road route between the Skew Bridge and the terminus. (J.Fozard)

FAIRYLAND
152

MANCHESTER SQUARE
PLEASURE BEACH
SOUTH PROM
BINGO
TATTOOIST
TWIN-CAR
PROMENADE

← 63. An interesting pre war scene at Central Pier, showing Standard car 153 on the Squires Gate service, with an open top streamliner in view. The Standards were replaced by the covered top streamlined double deckers on the Lytham Road route during 1935. The former Trocadero cinema is in the background.

↓ 64. This view looks south from the Central Station stop with part of the 'Golden Mile' of amusements and sideshows in the background. The station, in Bank Hey Street near the Tower, closed in 1964. On 28th October 1962, trailer car T10 (690), the last of the batch of 10 built in 1960 and hauled by towing car 280 (680) has just left the Central station tram stop and is about to be passed by double deck car 249 (712). T10, together with T8 and T9, were withdrawn in 1972. (C.W.Routh)

65. A busy scene at Central Station in 1936. A streamlined double decker heading south passes Lytham open top car 4 bound for the Gynn. In front of the Lytham car is a streamlined open top car. (W.J.Haynes)

METRO

Bus 709 Route TRAM Journey 1
Guard 6885 Ticket Number 735
Adult Single £1.60
St. Stephen's Ave
to
Waterloo Road
29/03/2008 12:10:35
Issued subject to published conditions
Enquiries: +44(0)1253 473001
blackpooltransport.com

An example of a 2008 tram ticket - see photograph 120.

66. Twin car 278 (678 hauling trailer T8 (688 passes the Central Static stop, with the promine Woolworths building and tl Tower in the backgroun In the early 1960s, the cars operated a limited sto service, the relevant stoppi places being displayed c the front of the car as show This twin set was one of tl three sets which were n reconfigured to the permane coupling and control trail arrangement, and T8 w scrapped in 1972, leaving 2' to operate alone. (D.F.Parke

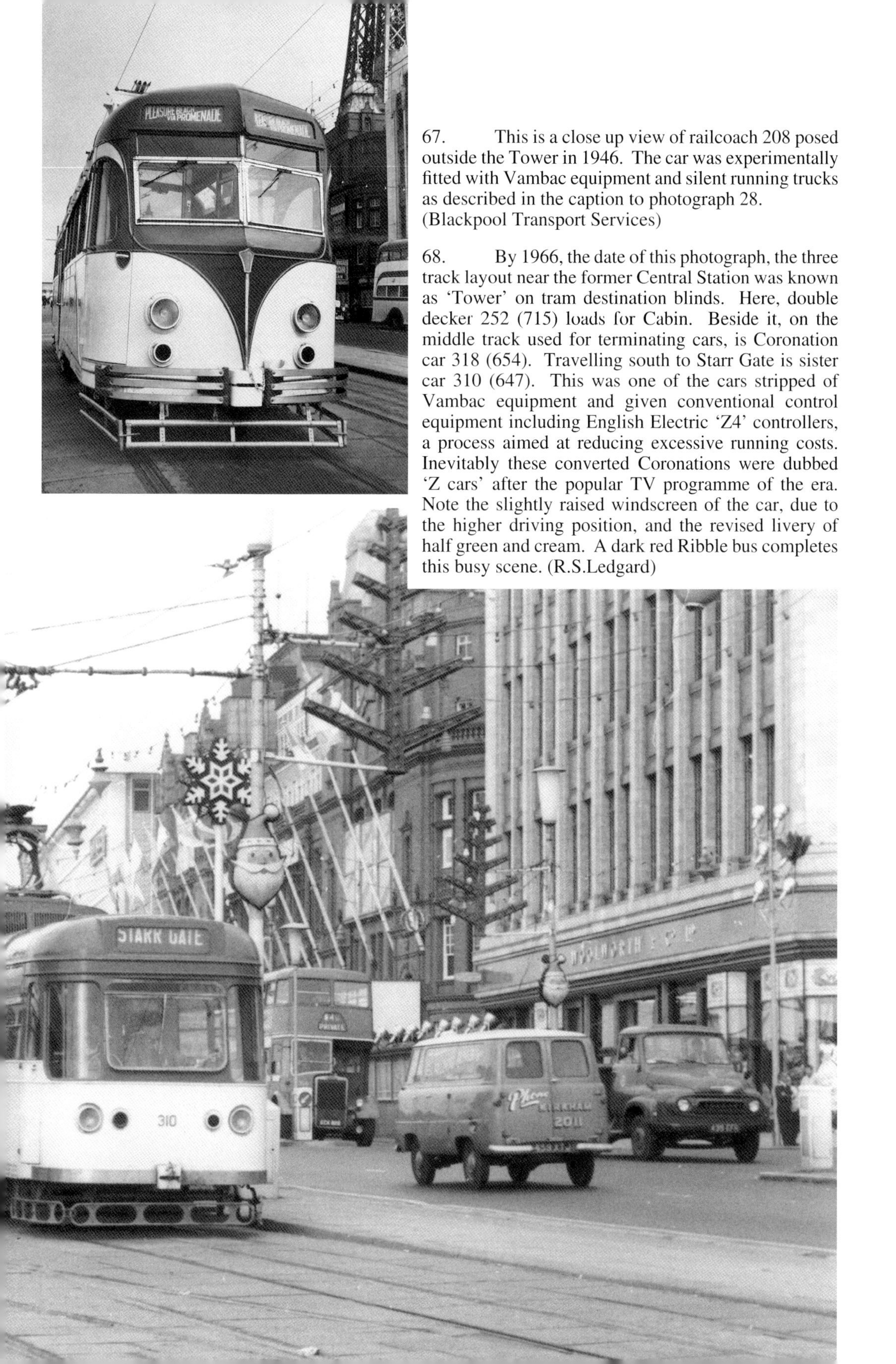

67. This is a close up view of railcoach 208 posed outside the Tower in 1946. The car was experimentally fitted with Vambac equipment and silent running trucks as described in the caption to photograph 28. (Blackpool Transport Services)

68. By 1966, the date of this photograph, the three track layout near the former Central Station was known as 'Tower' on tram destination blinds. Here, double decker 252 (715) loads for Cabin. Beside it, on the middle track used for terminating cars, is Coronation car 318 (654). Travelling south to Starr Gate is sister car 310 (647). This was one of the cars stripped of Vambac equipment and given conventional control equipment including English Electric 'Z4' controllers, a process aimed at reducing excessive running costs. Inevitably these converted Coronations were dubbed 'Z cars' after the popular TV programme of the era. Note the slightly raised windscreen of the car, due to the higher driving position, and the revised livery of half green and cream. A dark red Ribble bus completes this busy scene. (R.S.Ledgard)

69. The open top double deck streamlined cars operated a Promenade to Cleveleys service, for which a check rail was installed on the tramroad north of Bispham. This car, seen operating the service, is approaching North Pier from the south. (Lacey's Studios, Birmingham)

➔ 70. A short distance north of the Tower is the North Pier, facing Talbot Square. This is a key point on the tramway, and before 1962 was the interchange point with the Marton Service. A three track layout was installed here during the war to allow the many Promenade specials, operating between here and the Pleasure Beach, to terminate without affecting through cars. This interesting view from the immediate post war period shows a Sun Saloon car working on the Promenade, in the period before these cars were transferred to the Marton route. It has just arrived at North Pier, and the passengers are alighting. By this time these cars had been fully enclosed, and were being refurbished internally with cushioned seats and drivers' cabs. Note the connecting track from Talbot Square trailing in on the bottom right of this view.

NORTH PIER TO GYNN SQUARE

71 The Circular Tour, an extremely popular service operated with the open toastracks up to the very early years of the war, was revived in 1957 using the boat cars. These loaded on the second track in Talbot Square and then used the trailing connection onto the Promenade tracks to travel south to Starr Gate. From there they used the former Lytham Corporation tracks to connect to the Lytham Road route, returning to Talbot Square via Royal Oak and Marton. On 24th May 1959, boat car 227 (602) has departed from the Talbot Square loading point and is crossing onto the Promenade at the start of its one hour tour, whilst a sister car loads up behind. Note the advertising board, showing the price of the tour was then 1/3d (6½p). (R.B.Parr/National Tramway Museum)

72. This is a view of the three tracks in use at North Pier. A Coronation car on the middle track is flanked by two double deckers in this mid-1950s scene. (A.D.Packer)

TRAILER TRAMCAR OPERATION

In the operation of Trailer tramcars a number of questions arise, and the answers to the most obvious are as follows:—

"When"

. . . any door is open, all warning lights are illuminated, and the traction power is "OFF".

. . . the Motor Car Conductor signals START or STOP, a bell rings in the Driver's Cab.

. . . the Trailer Car Conductor signals START or STOP, a buzzer sounds in the Driver's cab.

. . . the Driver applies the AIR BRAKE all 16 wheels are braked.

73. By the early 1960s, most of the double deckers had received this mainly cream livery. This car is approaching the southbound unloading stop at North Pier on a journey to Starr Gate. The loading shelters for the Fleetwood service can be seen in the background. Note that in the intervening years since the previous photograph, the entry fee to the North Pier has risen from 3d (1 ½ p) to 6d (2 ½ p). The stars providing entertainment in 1962 at the North Pier include Harry Worth, Sheila Buxton, Bert Weedon and Billy Dainty. (J.Fozard)

74. Immediately north of North Pier, the tramway has to leave the Promenade diverting into the roadway to run behind the Metropole Hotel. Despite many schemes to run the trams around the seaward side of the hotel, this arrangement remains in force today. The tracks cross onto the roadway at an awkward angle and for years motorists have often been caught out by the intrusion of a tram. This early 1950s scene shows a Brush railcar approaching North Pier on a Promenade service, whilst a Warrington registered Morris 10 car nips round in front of it. (J.Fozard)

75. Coronation car 308 comes around the curve at the rear of the Metropole Hotel on 26th March, 1961. Note the 'Tram Pinch' sign on the left and the flats under construction on the other side of the road. (C.W.Routh)

➔ 76. Having negotiated the street track behind the Metropole Hotel, the tramway reverts to the Promenade reservation on the North Promenade. Road traffic has to veer to the right here, whilst the track proceeds straight on into the reservation. Many a motorist has followed a tram onto the paved tracks and today bollards are in place to prevent this. This unusual view looking south shows a double deck car about to pick up passengers at the Cocker Square stop. Note the typical Blackpool green 'Polo' tramstop. (J.Fozard)

➔ 77. This double deck car is negotiating the curve at the northern end of the North Promenade on 13th June 1954, having climbed the incline from Gynn Square, seen in the background. A railcoach is descending towards the Gynn on a Bispham service, and in the background, a 'Pantograph' car can be seen about to leave the Promenade turning into Dickson Road on the North Station service. Note the 'Maximum speed 4 mph' sign displayed on the left, protecting the service road onto the middle promenade which crosses the tracks at Gynn Square. (J.Fozard)

BUTLINS
STOP

NORTH STATION TO CABIN

78. The North Station to Fleetwood tram service was inherited from the Blackpool and Fleetwood Tramroad Company, taken over by the Corporation in 1920. Always known as route 1, and uniquely displayed as such on the cars, the service commenced at the Talbot Road end of Dickson Road, outside Blackpool North Railway Station. After 1920, a connection, involving interlaced track was made from Dickson Road turning right into Talbot Road and this connection to Talbot Square was maintained after the closure of the Layton tram service, being tarred over in 1949. The normal service was the sole responsibility of Bispham Depot, using their allocation of Brush railcars and railcoaches. This typical scene shows a Brush railcar at the terminus. The gabled building in the background is the Talbot Hotel, which had a bowling green at the rear. To the left of this, towering above the railway station, is Talbot Road bus station and car park, opened in 1939. Today the railway station has retreated eastwards and now comprises the site of the former excursion platforms. A Wilkinson's store occupies the former site.

79. Increasing traffic congestion, caused difficulties for guards turning the trolley at North Station. This resulted in the terminus being moved a short distance northwards to the Odeon cinema during the winter of 1960. A trolley reverser was erected here. This had to be carefully constructed to allow fixed head trolleys to be turned. The Brush railcar shown demonstrating the reversing manoeuvre is one of five Brush cars modified with a large single indicator between 1958 and 1962. These cars were 288, 291, 299, 300 and 301. Most of the remaining Brush cars were similarly treated during the 1970s. (J.Fozard)

80. Dickson Road runs from Talbot Road to Gynn Square. At the rear of the Carlton Hotel, with the Promenade only yards away to the left, a railcoach on route 1 is seen travelling north on the last day of operation of the service, 27th October 1963. (C.W.Routh)

81. In 1958, the provision of a check rail between Cleveleys and Fleetwood allowed double deckers to be used beyond the former point for the first time. These were then often used as extra cars on route 1 on Fleetwood market days. Prototype double decker 237 (700), in a unique mainly cream livery applied in 1962, is seen in Dickson Road behind the Derby Baths, having climbed up the hill from Gynn Square. Note the car is displaying 'North Station Blackpool'. It was only when working to this terminus that these cars showed 'Blackpool' on their screens. (J.Fozard)

TRAILER TRAMCAR OPERATION

"If"

. . . the service AIR BRAKE fails, normal rheostatic braking is still available, and also RESERVE EMERGENCY AIR BRAKING.

. . . the door controls at the platform fail, the doors can still be opened by duplicated controls, both INSIDE and OUTSIDE the Motor Car and Trailer Units.

. . . it is necessary to stop the vehicles without the aid of the driver, operation of either brake lever on the Conductor's platform will CUT OFF power and apply FULL AIR BRAKE PRESSURE to tram and trailer.

. . . the Trailer breaks away from the Motor Car, ALL BRAKES are AUTOMATICALLY APPLIED ON BOTH UNITS.

82. This April 1949 scene, with a Brush railcar in the wartime green livery, shows the car negotiating track repairs on the hill descending towards the Promenade at Gynn Square, which is in the background. (J.H.Meredith)

83. The importance of Gynn Square to the tramway is described in the caption to photograph 3. This elevated scene looking north towards the Cabin depicts the busy scene here just prior to the cessation of the Lytham St Annes tram service in April 1937 and shows the track layout which dated from 1924. A Lytham 'Pullman' car has just started to use the southern crossover, whilst a railcoach and an open top double decker wait for this movement to be completed. In the middle distance, painted in the recently introduced mainly cream livery, is a 'Pantograph' car climbing towards the Cabin. Following the loss of the Lytham cars, Gynn Square began to lose its importance as a tram terminus. The roadside loop, rarely used, was disconnected and later removed as was the south crossover. After the closure of the Dickson Road tramway, only the north crossover remained. Although this was sporadically used in emergencies and during engineering work, the crossover was removed as part of the 2008 track refurbishment and Gynn Square has now lost all of its special track facilities. (Geoff Smith coll.)

84. From Gynn Square the tracks climbed towards the Cabin, alongside the Sunken Gardens passing many of the popular hotels such as the Savoy and Cliffs. On 9th July 1960, 'Pantograph' car 171, in its last season in service, is negotiating the automatic points as it turns off the Promenade to proceed into Dickson Road. These cars were fitted with trolley ropes, and the few that survived into 1961 would have this feature removed so that they could use the newly installed trolley reverser at North Station. (A.D.Packer)

85. This railcoach is at the end of its journey to the Cabin, and the guard has alighted to set the points to enable the car to proceed onto the centre track. The deep dome at the car's end indicates that this car is the prototype railcoach 200, seen in the mid 1950s. It lasted in service until the end of the 1962 season. (W.J.Haynes)

86. The Cabin was at the summit of the line between Gynn Square and Bispham. The point is named after the long established hostelry called 'Uncle Tom's Cabin which since 1908 has been sited on the landward side of the Promenade. On the seaward side, a tower containing a lift was opened in 1930 to give access to the lower Promenade and the boating pool. This can be seen on the left of this view. The three track layout, which allowed the terminating service from Squires Gate to reverse without holding up through cars, dates from 1944. Previously a simple crossover was provided. This view dated 16th April 1949 shows all the tracks occupied. From left to right is railcoach 210, then double decker 251 (714) reversing to return to Lytham Road, and beside this is another railcoach, 202. Car 714 was withdrawn in 1971, but eventually formed the basis of the second Jubilee OMO double deck car 762 which entered service in 1982. (J.H.Meredith)

Stage Nos.

North Station—Fleetwood

Out	In																				North Station—Fleetwood
9	—																				NORTH STATION
10	—	2½																			EAVES STREET
11	44	2½	2½																		GYNN SQUARE
12	43	4	2½	2½																	CABIN
13	42	4	4	2½	2½																MINERS' HOME
14	41	5	4	4	2½	2½															BISPHAM
15	40	6	5	4	4	2½	2½														NORBRECK
16	39	7	6	5	4	4	2½	2½													LITTLE BISPHAM
17	38	8	7	6	5	5	4	2½	2½												ANCHORSHOLME CROSSING
18	37	8	8	7	6	6	5	4	2½	2½											CLEVELEYS
19	36	9	8	8	7	7	6	5	4	2½	2½										THORNTON GATE
20	35	9	9	8	8	7	6	5	5	4	2½	2½									ROSSALL BEACH
21	34	10	9	9	8	8	7	6	6	5	4	2½	2½								ROSSALL STATION
22	33	10	10	9	9	9	8	7	6	6	5	4	2½	2½							ROSSALL SQUARE
23	32	11	10	10	9	9	8	7	7	6	5	4	4	2½	2½						BROADWATER
24	31	1 -	11	10	10	10	9	8	7	7	6	5	4	4	2½	2½					LINGFIELD ROAD
25	30	1 -	1 -	11	10	10	9	8	8	7	7	6	5	5	4	2½	2½				STANLEY ROAD
26	29	1 1	1 -	1 -	11	11	10	9	8	8	7	7	6	6	5	4	2½	2½			ASH STREET
—	28	1 1	1 1	1 -	11	11	10	9	9	8	8	7	7	6	5	4	4	2½	2½		CHURCH STREET
—	27	1 1	1 1	1 -	1 -	1 -	11	10	9	9	8	8	7	6	6	5	4	4	2½	2½	FLEETWOOD

NOTE.—3d. MINIMUM ORDINARY FARE WILL OPERATE BETWEEN GYNN SQUARE AND BISPHAM FROM THE SATURDAY BEFORE WHITSUNTIDE UNTIL THE LAST DAY OF THE AUTUMN ILLUMINATIONS.

Coastal Tour

Stage Nos.		Fare	
1	CLIFTON DRIVE.	ADULTS	3 -
2	PLEASURE BEACH.	CHILDREN	1 6
3	CENTRAL STATION.		
4	TALBOT SQUARE.		
5	BISPHAM.		

87. Northwards from the Cabin, the paved track of the Promenade gives way to the sleeper track. The change of formation can be seen in the background to this view showing a Brush railcar on the left bound for Thornton Gate, and a terminating railcoach on the Squires Gate service. After 64 years, the three track layout has now reverted to the original single crossover layout as part of the 2008 track rationalisation (see photograph 120). (J.Fozard)

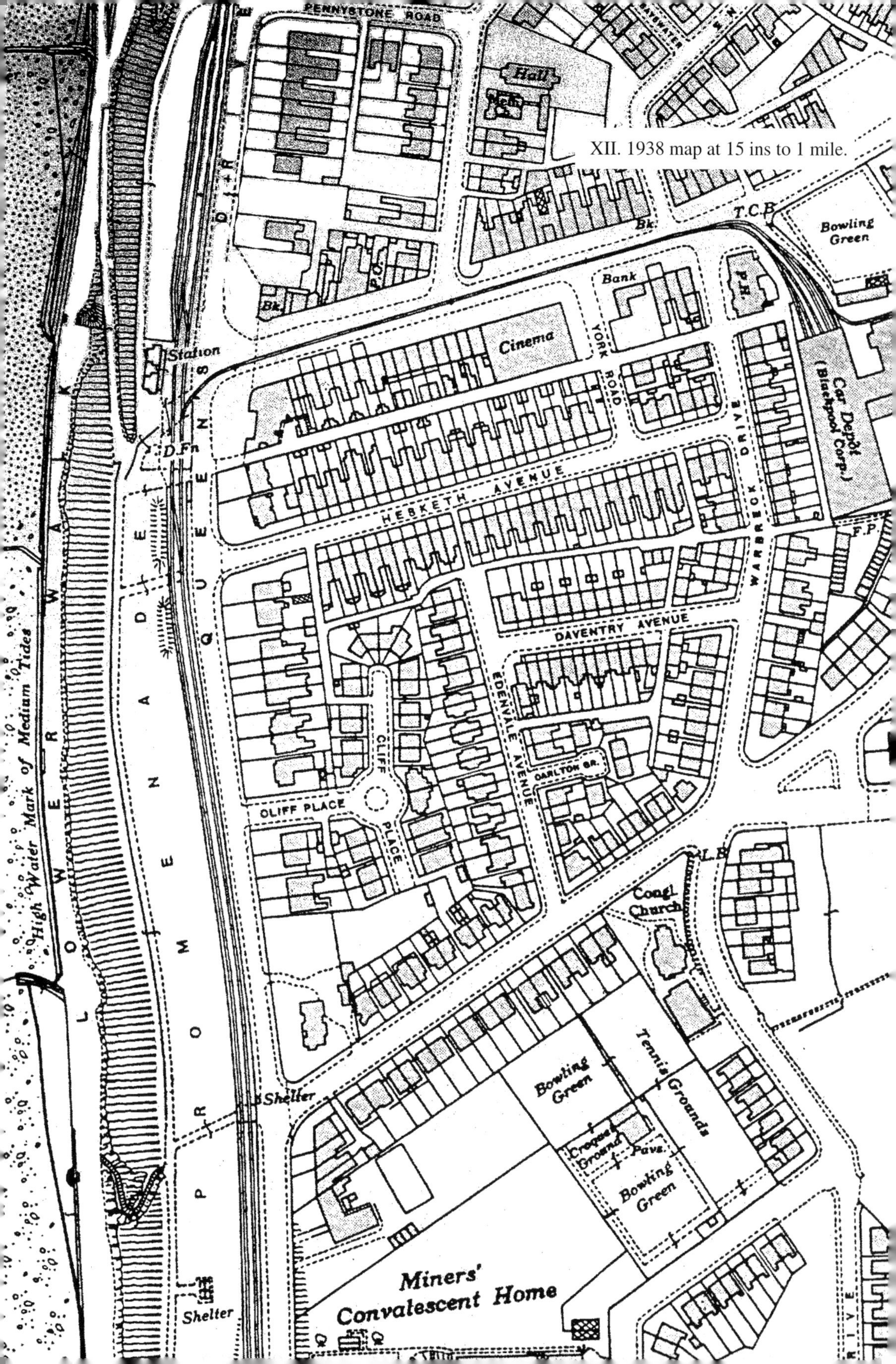

XII. 1938 map at 15 ins to 1 mile.

QUEENS PROMENADE AND BISPHAM

88. The sleeper track, running between the Queens Promenade and the cliffs above the Irish Sea, descends gently from the Cabin towards Bispham. This 1930s scene shows the reconstructed track along this section looking from St Stephen's Avenue with Bispham in the background. The typical neat concrete fencing is evident, as is the check rail to allow double deck operation. The most prominent landmark along this stretch is the Miners Home which is in the right background. The ground on the left beside the track is used every year to site the large Illumination displays. (Blackpool Transport Services)

89. A closer view of the Miners Home is seen in this scene showing railcoach 269 (616) proceeding south to Talbot Square. This large building, officially known as the 'Lancashire and Cheshire Miners Welfare Convalescent Home' was built in 1927 and opened by the Prince of Wales. It contained extensive indoor and outdoor recreational facilities including bowling greens, a billiards room and a cinema. The Home was one of only two of its type to be purpose built, the other being at Ingoldmells near Skegness. Closing in the 1980s, the building is now part of a luxury apartment complex known as Admiral Point. Rather like the Home, car 269, as 616, also had a new lease of life after withdrawal in 1970. It was totally rebuilt to become no 1, the first OMO car, entering service in this form in 1972, and was finally scrapped at the end of 1993.

90. This Brush railcar is approaching Bispham from the south on a route 1 journey to Cleveleys. The crossover in the foreground allowed access for cars from Bispham Depot proceeding northwards towards Fleetwood. It was removed after the closure of Bispham depot at the end of 1963. (Commercial postcard)

91. This is a general view of the tramway facilities at Bispham, looking north in about 1960. The Bispham Station building facing Red Bank Road is on the extreme left. In the centre are the two shelters for southbound cars, the nearest one is for route 1, whilst the other is for Promenade cars. Through the typical Blackpool welcome arch can be seen a Brush railcar crossing Queens Promenade to enter service, having run up Red Bank Road from Bispham depot. On the right are the Queens Mansions private flats, built in the late 1930s and sometimes used by the variety stars appearing in Blackpool. Today, Queens Mansions is comprised of upmarket holiday apartments. (Commercial postcard)

RED BANK ROAD

92. The single track tramway along Red Bank Road led to Bispham depot. Originally this was the main running depot of the Blackpool and Fleetwood Tramroad, dating from 1898. It had six roads and capacity for 36 single deck cars. Its original role was continued in Blackpool Corporation days, providing all the scheduled cars for the route 1 service, as well as some for the Promenade service. In the late 1950s until 1961 its cars also ran on the Squires Gate to Bispham service. All the Pantograph cars and Brush railcars were housed here, together with a few railcoaches. In this 1957 view, Brush railcar 303 is about to turn right into the depot yard. The large house in the distance is the Bispham Conservative Club, originally the home of the General Manager of the Tramroad Company. The site of the depot, which closed operationally on 27th October 1963, and was vacated by early 1966, is now a Sainsbury's supermarket. On the extreme right is the Bispham Hotel, whose pub sign today shows a streamlined double decker, even though these cars were too large to run from Bispham depot. Car 303, previously described in the caption to photograph 28, was the experimental car fitted with Vambac control and rarely seen in service. Note the lack of destination indicator over the car's entrance, the additional louvres at the base of the trolley tower, where the Vambac equipment was situated, and the lack of a controller handle, normally a prominent feature able to be easily seen through the windscreens of Brush cars. The car was withdrawn in 1962. (A.D.Packer)

93. A close up of a Brush railcar at the top of Red Bank Road (known as 'Bispham top'), and crossing onto the Promenade under the watchful eye of the constable on point duty. Although this road junction is today controlled by traffic lights, on busy Illumination weekends, manual traffic control by point duty officers is still necessary. Behind the tram in the centre background is the Café Royal, a long established business which still trades today. (J Fozard)

➔ 94. A view showing the same point as the previous photograph, but looking towards the sea, shows railcoach 202 crossing Queens Promenade from Red Bank Road. Bispham tram station is prominent in the background. This provided facilities for an inspector's office and crew accommodation for cashing in and replenishment of tea cans. The track and overhead in Red Bank Road was removed in early 1966 and today no trace of it remains. (J.Fozard)

➔ 95. This interesting snapshot, taken from Bispham Station in wartime, shows cream liveried 'Pantograph' car 174 working northwards on route 1. This livery was intended to make these cars look as similar as possible to the new railcoaches, even to the extent of placing the fleet numbers above the centre windows, although these were transfers rather than the metal 'house numbers' fitted to the railcoaches. Behind the tram is Queens Mansions, and the overhead wiring curving round from Red Bank Road can be seen. It appears that hoods have been placed over the ears supporting the tram wire, presumably to hide electrical flashes during blackout conditions.

LADIES
TALBOT SQUARE
QUEENS PROMENADE

TOWARDS NORBRECK AND LITTLE BISPHAM

96. Immediately north of Bispham station the track formation runs into a cutting and widens, to allow a lengthy three track section. The middle track is used to reverse cars terminating here, and also to park here if necessary for crew meal breaks. Up to 2007, two crossovers were provided but the 2008 track rebuilding has resulted in only one now remaining. This point, being the northerly limit of the Illuminations, could get very busy with trams, and still is today, especially on autumn weekends. Seen here on 13th May 1966 are two interesting cars. To the right on the centre track is newly rebuilt railcoach 264 (611), now resembling a trailer towing car and incorporating exterior 'Darvic' panelling. This material was a plastic laminate normally used for vehicle interior lining panels. It was dubbed the 'plastic tram' and had a reputation for speed, running in this form until it was again rebuilt into OMO car 12 during the 1970s. Passing by on the left is Coronation car 328 (664), the last of the batch, which since late 1964 had lost its Vambac equipment and was running with conventional Z4 controllers. (L.G.Sidwell)

97. A mid 1950s view from above the cutting at Bispham, showing sunbathers on the grassy cliff top. A Coronation car, still retaining frontal chrome strips, waits on the centre track before returning to Central Station. (Geoff Smith coll.)

98. A late 1930s panorama looking from an upper floor of Queens Mansions, shows the cliff top coastline and tramway stretching away towards Norbreck and Cleveleys. Amongst the trams in view are two open top double deckers returning from Cleveleys or Little Bispham. Note that the hotels along the Promenade still have gardens, a feature long gone due to the desire to accommodate the private car. (Geoff Smith coll.)

99. At Norbreck, the cliff top is dominated by the castellated Norbreck Hydropathic Hotel, now the Norbreck Castle Hotel, which continues to provid useful traffic for the tramway. The motor road beside the tramway was opened in 1932 between Norbreck and Anchorsholme, and was the final link of the coast road between Blackpool and Cleveleys. Coronation car 308 (645) is near the end of its journey to Little Bispham and is being passed by a railcoach on route 1. Norbreck tram station is in the right background. (R.F.Mack)

100. Looking north from Norbreck a railcoach with cream windscreen surrounds, approaches Little Bispham, where the brick built station can be seen in the background. On the right are the flats at Norkeed Court. (J.Fozard)

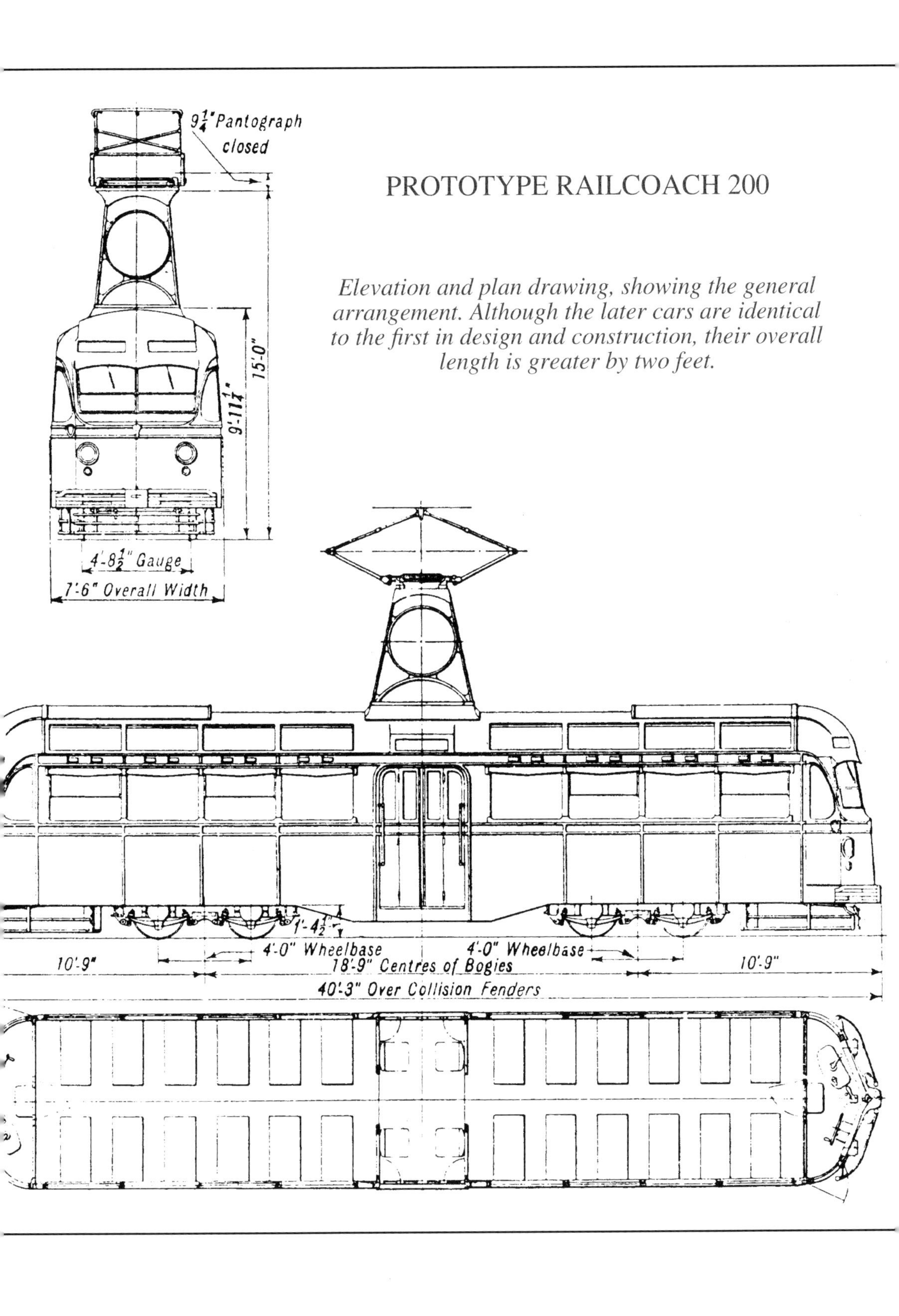

PROTOTYPE RAILCOACH 200

Elevation and plan drawing, showing the general arrangement. Although the later cars are identical to the first in design and construction, their overall length is greater by two feet.

101. A short distance north of Little Bispham station is the large Little Bispham turning circle which was brought into use in June 1938. This provision eased the congestion caused by cars reversing at Bispham. It became particularly useful after the introduction of the 'Twin cars', which initially could not reverse, and again from the 1970s onwards with the introduction of one man cars, where reversal involving the driver changing ends was not considered desirable for security reasons. In this view dated 13th June 1954, double deck car 258 (721) waits at the exit to the circle before commencing a journey to Squires Gate, whilst boat car 229 stands on the spur track giving access to the northbound track during an enthusiasts' tour. This connection, removed in 2008, was little used except during the Illuminations, when a works car was routinely stationed on this track in readiness for any emergency. (R.J.S.Wiseman)

Stage Nos.

Squires Gate—Bispham—Thornton Gate

Out	In																		
1	—	SQUIRES GATE																	
2	—	2½	HIGHFIELD ROAD																
3	51	2½	2½	WATSON ROAD															
5	50	4	2½	2½	ROYAL OAK														
6	49	4	4	2½	2½	MANCHESTER SQUARE													
7	48	5	5	4	2½	2½	CENTRAL PIER												
8	47	6	5	4	4	2½	2½	CENTRAL STATION											
9	46	6	6	5	4	4	2½	2½	TALBOT SQUARE										
10	45	7	7	6	5	4	4	2½	2½	PLEASANT STREET									
11	44	8	8	7	6	5	5	4	2½	2½	GYNN SQUARE								
12	43	8	8	7	7	6	5	4	4	2½	2½	CABIN							
13	42	9	9	8	7	7	6	5	4	4	2½	2½	MINERS' HOME						
14	41	9	9	8	8	7	7	6	5	4	4	2½	2½	BISPHAM STATION					
15	40	10	10	9	8	8	8	7	6	5	4	4	2½	2½	NORBRECK				
16	39	11	11	10	9	8	8	8	7	6	5	4	4	2½	2½	LITTLE BISPHAM			
17	38	1 -	1 -	11	10	9	9	8	8	7	6	5	5	4	2½	2½	ANCHORSHOLME CROSSING		
—	37	1 -	1 -	11	10	10	10	9	8	8	7	6	6	5	4	2½	2½	CLEVELEYS	
—	36	1 1	1 1	1/-	11	10	10	9	9	8	8	7	7	6	5	4	2½	2½	THORNTON GATE

NOTE.—3d. MINIMUM ORDINARY FARE WILL OPERATE BETWEEN MANCHESTER SQUARE AND BISPHAM FROM THE SATURDAY BEFORE WHITSUNTIDE TO THE LAST DAY OF THE AUTUMN ILLUMINATIONS.

Children between 3 and 15 years of age are charged as follows : 1½d. for 2½d. fares ; 2d. for 3d., 3½d. and 4d. fares ; 2½d. for 4½d. fares ; 3d. for 5d. and 6d. fare 4d. for 7d. and 8d. fares ; 5d. for 9d. and 10d. fares ; 6d. for 11d. and 1/- fares ; 7d. for 1/1d. and 1/2d. fares ; 8d. for 1/3d. and 1/4d. fares ; 9d. for 1/5d. and 1/6d. fa

DOGS.—For dogs the fares are as adult passenger fares, with a maximum of 4d.

ANCHORSHOLME AND CLEVELEYS

102. Beyond Little Bispham, the tramroad drops down to Anchorsholme junction on the outskirts of Cleveleys. Brush railcar 299 (636) is seen here in 1962, newly repainted with cream windscreen surrounds and newly fitted single destination indicators. The car is waiting at the traffic lights before crossing to the side reservation and climbing the hill to Little Bispham. From here to Cleveleys town centre, the track is on a central reservation between the two road carriageways. (J.Fozard)

103. The central Cleveleys tram stop was at the junction with Victoria Road. Brush railcar 294 (631) is seen crossing through the traffic roundabout here on a journey terminating at Cleveleys on 6th September 1964. The roundabout was later removed and replaced by multi-phased traffic signals. (L.G.Sidwell)

104. Despite there being regular cars reversing here, the track layout at Cleveleys only consists of a simple crossover. Until 1958, when a check rail was provided through to Fleetwood, this point was the northerly limit of operation for double deck tramcars. This view dated June 1953 shows a Brush railcar on route 1 heading for North Station and a double deck car about to reverse to return to Squires Gate. Note the Coronation plaque on the trolley tower of the railcar. (J.Fozard)

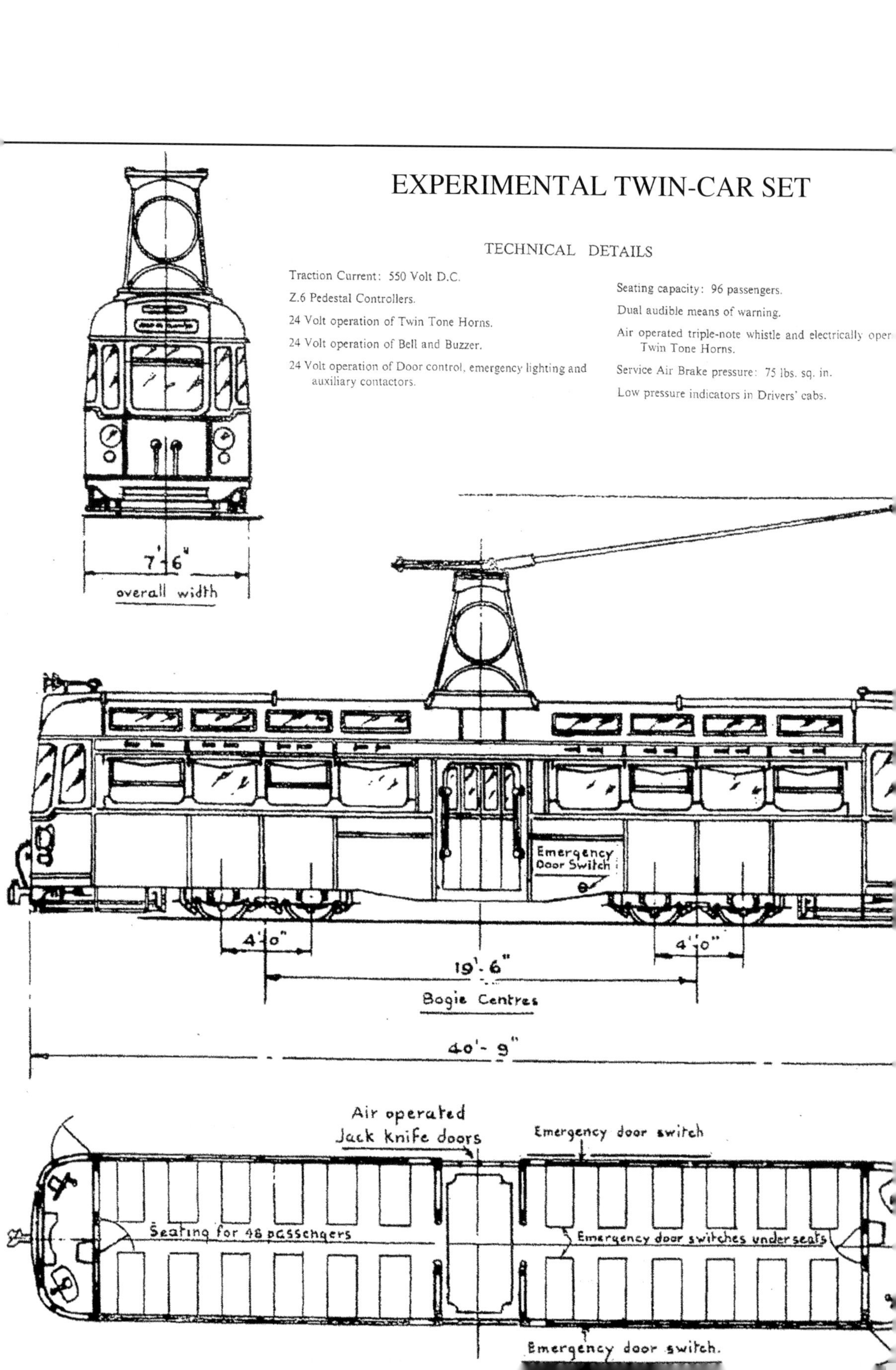
EXPERIMENTAL TWIN-CAR SET
TECHNICAL DETAILS
Traction Current: 550 Volt D.C.
Z.6 Pedestal Controllers.
24 Volt operation of Twin Tone Horns.
24 Volt operation of Bell and Buzzer.
24 Volt operation of Door control, emergency lighting and auxiliary contactors.
Seating capacity: 96 passengers.
Dual audible means of warning.
Air operated triple-note whistle and electrically oper
Twin Tone Horns.
Service Air Brake pressure: 75 lbs. sq. in.
Low pressure indicators in Drivers' cabs.
7'-6"
overall width
Emergency Door Switch
4'-0"
4'-0"
19'-6"
Bogie Centres
40'-9"
Air operated
Jack Knife doors
Emergency door switch
Seating for 48 passengers
Emergency door switches under seats
Emergency door switch.

105. The programme of permanently coupling the Twin cars, and providing a driving cab in the trailers, considerably improved these cars' flexibility of operation. This is demonstrated here, in this view of 'Twin car' set 272 (672) and T2 (682) reversing on the Cleveleys crossover,being driven from the trailer car. The date is 29th May 1966. (L.G.Sidwell)

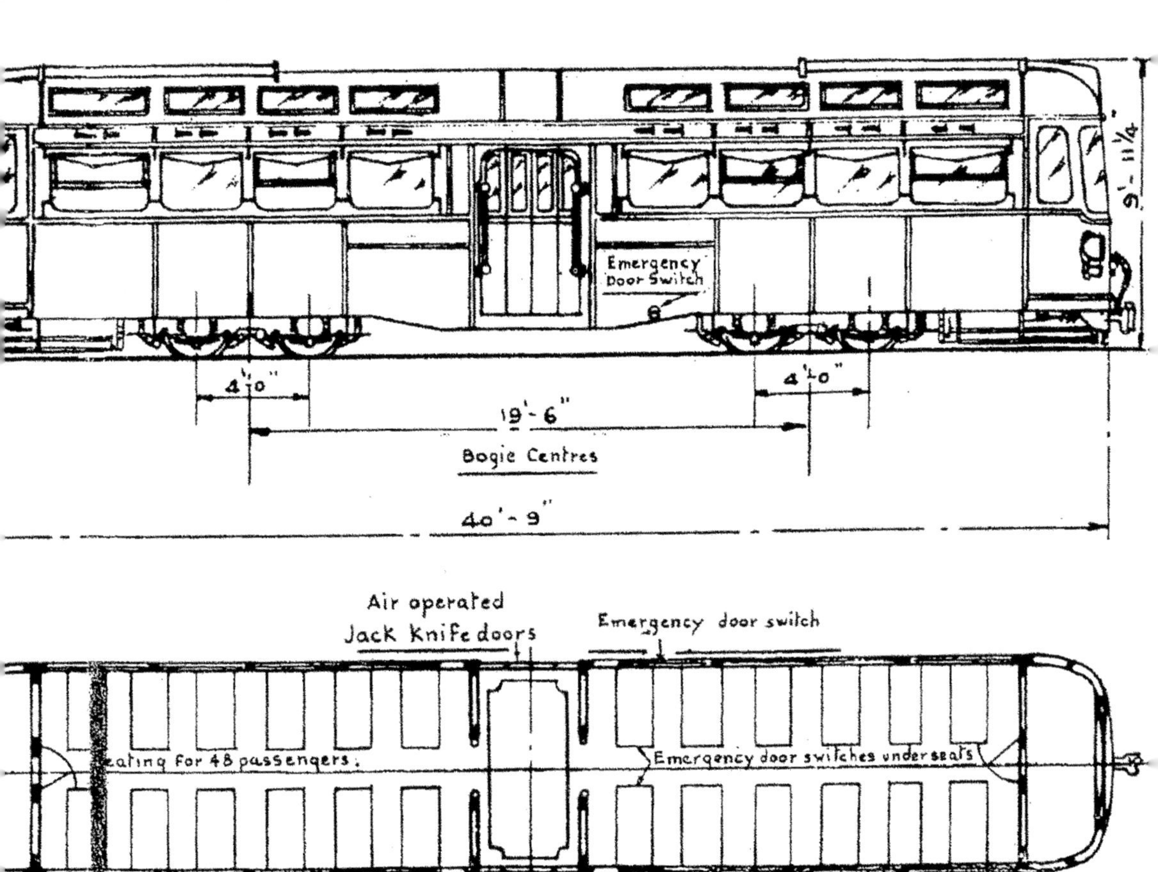

106. Northwards from Cleveleys, the track runs on a side reservation, with several side roads crossing the track, thereby reducing the running speed of the cars. Railcoach 268 (615) is operating southbound and approaching the Stockdove Way crossing. Travelling northbound is railcoach 270 (617). This view was taken on Boxing Day 1963 in the period when the tramway was closed for the winter as an economy measure except for the Cleveleys to Fleetwood section. An eight minute tram service was maintained on this section, with passengers transferring to buses at Cleveleys. Both railcoaches seen here were rebuilt in the 1970s, becoming OMO cars 11 and 6 respectively. (L.G.Sidwell)

ALL STOPS TO FLEETWOOD

107. Thornton Gate marks the northern edge of Cleveleys, and the tram station here saw a regular service of terminating cars. Here, there was also an area of sidings to where there were regular deliveries of coal from Fleetwood, using the Corporation's electric locomotive. This service ceased in 1949 and the sidings were later used as a permanent way store. A three track layout was provided on the main running lines. In 1953, Coronation car 316 (652) passes the station building (note the waiting room sign on the extreme left) en route to Fleetwood. Visible in the sidings on the right is a permanent way car, formerly 'Fleetwood rack' 127, which was later restored for the tramway's 75th anniversary in 1960 and returned to service as Tramroad car 2. It now resides, in full working order at the National Tramway Museum at Crich. In the 1960s many of the original railcoaches were dismantled in the sidings, and later some of the Coronation cars. (W.J.Haynes)

108. Near Rossall, a siding was constructed in the early war years to accommodate trams carrying troops to and from the nearby rifle range. The Sun saloon cars 10 to 21 were normally used for this work. Coronation car 319 (655) passes the siding on a southbound journey, just after departing from Rossall station. In 1970 this car lost its Vambac equipment and was converted to operate with conventional controllers. This was the thirteenth and last car to be so treated. (D.F.Parker)

STARR GATE
305
ROSSALL

ROSSALL SQUARE

← 109. The typical tramroad station at Rossall, is located on the deviation to the original route between Rossall and Broadwater. This was brought into use in 1925 before the Broadway motor road was built, and it cut 300 yards off the length of the line, as well as avoiding a very sharp curve. Coronation car 305 (642) pauses here 24th October 1966 on a southbound journey before crossing Rossall Lane. (L.G.Sidwell)

← 110. Beyond Rossall, the tramroad curves away from the main road and runs alongside the fields. Railcoach 283 (620) passes the Rossall Square stop on a journey to Fleetwood on 27th December 1963. Today, housing has encroached to the edge of the tramroad and this rural aspect has largely disappeared. This railcoach was numerically the last of its type and became OMO car 2 in the 1970s. (L.G.Sidwell)

111. The crossover at Broadwater was at the Blackpool side of the road crossing, and was regularly used by the local tram service from Fleetwood that ran on market days. In this scene from March 1961, Fleetwood 'Box' car 40, one of the historic cars restored to service for the tramway's 75th anniversary in 1960, has just used the crossover, clearing the road for railcoach 206 to proceed towards Fleetwood. Note that, although a cross wire was provided for reversing trams, this was not linked by a frog to the main wires. (C.W.Routh)

112. The station at Broadwater is seen here with railcoach 264 (611) proceeding south towards Cleveleys on 27th December 1963. The tramroad crosses Fleetwood Road at this point. Note the compulsory 'Polo' type stop sign 'All cars stop here'. This car was rebuilt as the 'plastic tram' in 1966 (see photograph 96). (L.G.Sidwell)

113. North of Broadwater, the tramroad enters Fleetwood on a reserved track sandwiched between Radcliffe Road and Copse Road. Here, at Stanley Road, Copse Road depot was situated, built by the Tramroad company. It was never used as a running shed, but housed the company's crossbench cars used only in the summer. There were originally six roads, giving a capacity of 18 cars. A track also led to a connection with the Poulton to Fleetwood railway, which ran behind the depot. In Corporation days, this connection was used by the electric locomotive to collect loaded coal trucks for delivery to Thornton Gate sidings. The permanent way department was also moved to here. The building was cleared in 1963 and sold. It still exists and is in use as a car dealer's premises. This 1938 view is taken from the depot looking across to the houses in Radcliffe Road. New Brush railcar 300 passes en route to Fleetwood.

114. The reserved track ends at Ash Street, where the tramway runs onto street track for the final mile to the terminus. Looking back towards the reserved track, with Radcliffe Road on the right, Coronation 317 (653) picks up passengers at Ash Street station on 29th May 1966, before returning to Blackpool, despite what is shown on the car's destination indicator. (L.G.Sidwell)

FLEETWOOD: STREET RUNNING

115. This scene looks north along Fleetwood's main street, Lord Street. The Ash Street crossover was at the south end just off the reserved track. Reversing a car here was awkward because of the lack of a cross wire. This railcoach has driven onto the crossover with its trolley pole leading and the guard is now swinging the pole into the correct position on the southbound wire. (Geoff Smith)

116. At the north end of Lord Street, the tracks swing left outside St Peters Church into North Albert Street. On a murky 28th December 1963, railcoach 271 (618) picks up passengers near the end of Lord Street with the Church in the background during the period when trams were only running between Fleetwood and Cleveleys. This car was rebuilt with tapered ends in the late 1960s, and later became OMO car 13. (L.G.Sidwell)

FLEETWOOD FERRY

117. At the northern end of North Albert Street, the tramway makes a one way loop to the Ferry terminus alongside Fleetwood Pier. Here connections can be made to the Knott End Ferry or in former times to the seasonal steamers to the Isle of Man. The terminal loop was brought into use in 1925. Previously the tramway terminated at the end of North Albert Street at Bold Street, near the Cottage Hospital. In Tramway Company days, there was a small depot at the end of the line beside the North Euston Hotel. This had two roads and held four cars. It was never used by the Corporation and the building was demolished in 1973. At the ferry terminus there is a loop in the wide roadway. In view is 'Pantograph' car 168 beside a double deck streamliner, a scene only possible after 1958. A railcar, with strings of bulbs strung from the trolley tower, brings up the rear. Car 168 is working as far as Cleveleys only. On busy market days, these cars regularly operated 'local' journeys for the benefit of residents, most commonly to Broadwater. The black smoke in the background suggests that a ship may be hidden behind the trams – the deep water channel is very close to the shore at this point.

118. Looking east, this view shows Fleetwood railway station in the background. The railway closed in 1966 and the building is now demolished. A Coronation car is seen on special duties beside 'Pantograph' 168 which is waiting to depart for North Station in 1953. (J.Fozard)

119. Leaving the Ferry terminus, trams turn sharp right into Pharos Street, which is dominated by the 90 feet high lighthouse, officially known as the Fleetwood High Light. This is sited literally in the middle of the street. Having passed beside the tower, Coronation 315 (651) is seen turning back into North Albert Street, completing its journey around the terminal loop on its almost 12 mile journey back through Blackpool to Starr Gate. (J.Fozard)

Streamliners in 2008

120. This photograph brings the story up to the year 2008. Extensive track rebuilding necessitated, for the first time ever, the complete closure of the tramway after the end of the 2007 season in November. Partial reopening occurred on Good Friday 19th March 2008, when a service resumed between Starr Gate and Cabin. The full line was opened on Saturday 26th April. This view shows Cabin terminus on Saturday 29th March 2008. Car 709, formerly 246, was rebuilt into this form in 2000, one of four similar cars given this treatment. The all over advertising is a concept that was unheard of in the 1930s. Note the barriers, preventing any operation north of Cabin. The car is about to reverse on the new crossover which replaces the former three track layout. The numerous poles seen on the right are used to support the Illumination features which every autumn line the trackside between here and Bispham.

Present number	Pre-1968 number	Year built	Type	Current status
600	225	1934	Boat 1930s livery *Duchess of Cornwall*	
602	227	1934	Boat	Operational
604	230	1934	Boat	Operational
605	233	1934	Boat	Operational
607	236	1934	Boat	Stored
619	(282)	1987	Vanguard covered toastrack. (OMO car 7).	Stored
621	284	1937	Brush railcar	Stored
622	285	1937	Brush railcar	Operational
623	286	1937	Brush railcar. Restored to wartime livery.	Operational
625	288	1937	Brush railcar	Stored
626	289	1937	Brush railcar	Operational
627	290	1937	Brush railcar	Stored
630	293	1937	Brush railcar	Operational
631	294	1937	Brush railcar	Operational
632	295	1937	Brush railcar	Stored
634	297	1937	Brush railcar	Stored
636	299	1937	Brush railcar	Away
637	300	1937	Brush railcar	Stored
(641)	304	1952	Coronation Vambac (Lancastrian Transport Trust)	Operational
660	324	1953	Coronation 'Z car'	Operational
671	281	1935	Towing car Rebuilt from railcoach 1960.	Operational
672	272	1935	Towing car Rebuilt from railcoach 1960.	Operational
673	273	1935	Towing car Rebuilt from railcoach 1961.	Operational
674	274	1935	Towing car Rebuilt from railcoach 1962.	Operational
675	275	1935	Towing car Rebuilt from railcoach 1958. Trailer 1958-61	Operational
676	276	1935	Towing car Rebuilt from railcoach 1958.	Stored
678	278	1935	Towing car Rebuilt from railcoach 1961. Single car.	Stored
679	279	1935	Towing car Rebuilt from railcoach 1961. Single car.	Stored
680	280	1935	Towing car Rebuilt from railcoach 1960. Single car.	Operational
681	T1	1960	Trailer car Attached to car 671.	Operational
682	T2	1960	Trailer car Attached to car 672.	Operational
683	T3	1960	Trailer car Attached to car 673.	Operational
684	T4	1960	Trailer car Attached to car 674.	Operational
685	T5	1960	Trailer car Attached to car 675.	Operational
686	T6	1960	Trailer car Attached to car 676.	Stored
687	T7	1960	Trailer car Unattached.	Stored.
700	237	1934	Double deck. Restored 1996 to Wartime condition.	Operational
701	238	1934	Double deck	Operational
702	239	1934	Double deck	Operational
703	240	1934	Double deck	Operational
704	241	1934	Double deck	Stored
706	243	1934	Double deck. Rebuilt to open top 1985. *Princess Alice.*	Operational
707	244	1934	Double deck. Rebuilt 1998.	Operational
708	245	1934	Double deck	Stored
709	246	1934	Double deck. Rebuilt 2000.	Operational
710	247	1934	Double deck	Operational
711	248	1934	Double deck	Operational
712	249	1934	Double deck	Operational
713	250	1934	Double deck	Operational
715	252	1935	Double deck	Operational
716	253	1935	Double deck	Stored
717	254	1935	Double deck. Rebuilt 2008 to original condition.	Operational
718	255	1935	Double deck. Rebuilt 2002.	Operational
719	256	1935	Double deck. Former Walls tram	Operational.
720	257	1935	Double deck	Stored
721	258	1935	Double deck	Operational
722	259	1935	Double deck	Stored
723	260	1935	Double deck	Operational
724	261	1935	Double deck. Rebuilt 2004.	Operational
726	263	1935	Double deck	Operational
733	(209)	1962	Illuminated - locomotive. Rebuilt from railcoach 209.	Stored
737	296	2001	Illuminated trawler. Rebuilt from railcar 633.	Operational
761	262	1979	Jubilee double deck car Rebuilt from car 725.	Operational
762	251	1982	Jubilee double deck car Rebuilt from car 714. *Stuart L Pillar*	Operational

Other cars in fleet 2008

641 to 648	Built 1984-88	Centenary cars	Operational
732	Built 1961	Rocket ex Pantograph car168	Stored
734	Built 1962	Western carriage ex car 174	Stored
736	Built 1965	Warship ex Pantograph car 170	Operational
Stockport 5	Built 1901	Vintage car on long term loan	Operational
B & F 40	Built 1914	Vintage car on long term loan	Operational
Bolton 66	Built 1901	Vintage car on long term loan	Operational
147	Built 1924	Blackpool Standard car *Michael Airey*	Operational
Sheffield 513	Built 1952	Vintage car on long term loan	Operational

Trolley poles are fitted to cars:
600 to 607, 706, 717, 304, 660 plus 732, 5, 40, 66, 147, 513. All other cars have pantographs

EVOLVING THE ULTIMATE RAIL ENCYCLOPEDIA

Easebourne Lane, Midhurst, West Sussex.
GU29 9AZ Tel:01730 813169
www.middletonpress.co.uk email:info@middletonpress.co.uk
A-978 0 906520 B- 978 1 873793 C- 978 1 901706 D-978 1 904474 E - 978 1 906008

OOP Out of print at time of printing - Please check availability BROCHURE AVAILABLE SHOWING NEW TITLES

A
Abergavenny to Merthyr C 91 8
Abertillery and Ebbw Vale Lines D 84 5
Aldgate & Stepney Tramways B 70 1
Allhallows - Branch Line to A 62 8
Alton - Branch Lines to A 11 6
Andover to Southampton A 82 6
Ascot - Branch Lines around A 64 2
Ashburton - Branch Line to B 95 4
Ashford - Steam to Eurostar B 67 1
Ashford to Dover A 48 2
Austrian Narrow Gauge D 04 3
Avonmouth - BL around D 42 5
Aylesbury to Rugby D 91 3
B
Baker Street to Uxbridge D 90 6
Banbury to Birmingham D 27 2
Barking to Southend C 80 2
Barnet & Finchley Tramways B 93 0
Barry - Branch Lines around D 50 0
Bath Green Park to Bristol C 36 9
Bath to Evercreech Junction A 60 4
Bath Tramways B 86 2
Battle over Portsmouth 1940 A 29 1
Battle over Sussex 1940 A 79 6
Bedford to Wellingborough D 31 9
Betwixt Petersfield & Midhurst A 94 9
Birmingham to Wolverhampton E 25 3
Birmingham Trolleybuses E 19 2
Bletchley to Cambridge D 94 4
Bletchley to Rugby E 07 9
Blitz over Sussex 1941-42 B 35 0
Bodmin - Branch Lines around B 83 1
Bognor at War 1939-45 B 59 6
Bombers over Sussex 1943-45 B 51 0
Bournemouth & Poole Trys B 47 3
Bournemouth to Evercreech Jn A 46 8
Bournemouth to Weymouth A 57 4
Bournemouth Trolleybuses C 10 9
Bradford Trolleybuses D 19 7
Brecon to Neath D 43 2
Brecon to Newport D 16 6
Brecon to Newtown E 06 2
Brighton to Eastbourne A 16 1
Brighton to Worthing A 03 1
Brighton Trolleybuses D 34 0
Bristols Tramways B 57 2
Bristol to Taunton D 03 6
Bromley South to Rochester B 23 7
Bromsgrove to Birmingham D 87 6
Bromsgrove to Gloucester D 73 9
Brunel - A railtour of his achievements D 74 6
Bude - Branch Line to B 29 9
Burnham to Evercreech Jn A 68 0
Burton & Ashby Tramways C 51 2
C
Camberwell & West Norwood Tys B 22 0
Cambridge to Ely D 55 5
Canterbury - Branch Lines around B 58 9
Cardiff Trolleybuses D 64 7
Caterham & Tattenham Corner B 25 1
Changing Midhurst C 15 4
Chard and Yeovil - BLs around C 30 7
Charing Cross to Dartford A 75 8
Charing Cross to Orpington A 96 3
Cheddar - Branch Line to B 90 9
Cheltenham to Andover C 43 7
Cheltenham to Redditch D 81 4
Chesterfield Tramways D 37 1
Chesterfield Trolleybuses D 51 7
Chester Tramways E 04 8
Chichester to Portsmouth A 14 7
Clapham & Streatham Trys B 97 8
Clapham Junction to Beckenham Jn B 36 7
Cleobury Mortimer - BLs around E 18 5
Clevedon & Portishead - BLs to D 18 0
Collectors Trains, Trolleys & Trams D 29 6
Colonel Stephens D62 3
Cornwall Narrow Gauge D 56 2
Cowdray & Easebourne D 96 8
Crawley to Littlehampton A 34 5
Cromer - Branch Lines around C 26 0
Croydons Tramways B 42 8
Croydons Trolleybuses B 73 2
Croydon to East Grinstead B 48 0
Crystal Palace (HL) & Catford Loop A 87 1
Cyprus Narrow Gauge E13 0
D
Darlington - Leamside - Newcastle E 28 4
Darlington to Newcastle D 98 2
Darlington Trolleybuses D 33 3
Dartford to Sittingbourne B 34 3
Derby Tramways D 17 3
Derby Trolleybuses C 72 7
Derwent Valley - Branch Line to the D 06 7
Devon Narrow Gauge E 09 3
Didcot to Banbury D 02 9
Didcot to Swindon C 84 0
Didcot to Winchester C 13 0
Dorset & Somerset Narrow Gauge D 76 0
Douglas to Peel C 88 8
Douglas to Port Erin C 55 0
Douglas to Ramsey D 39 5
Dovers Tramways B 24 4
Dover to Ramsgate A 78 9
Dunstable - Branch Lines to E 27 7
E
Ealing to Slough C 42 0
East Cornwall Mineral Railways D 22 7
East Croydon to Three Bridges A 53 6
East Grinstead - Branch Lines to A 07 9
East Ham & West Ham Tramways B 52 7
East London - Branch Lines of C 44 4
East London Line B 80 0
East Ridings Secret Resistance D 21 0
Edgware & Willesden Tramways C 18 5
Effingham Junction - BLs around A 74 1
Ely to Norwich C 90 1
Embankment & Waterloo Tramways B 41 1
Enfield Town & Palace Gates - BL to D 32 6
Epsom to Horsham A 30 7
Euston to Harrow & Wealdstone C 89 5
Exeter & Taunton Tramways B 32 9
Exeter to Barnstaple B 15 2
Exeter to Newton Abbot C 49 9
Exeter to Tavistock B 69 5
Exmouth - Branch Lines to B 00 8
F
Fairford - Branch Line to A 52 9
Falmouth, Helston & St. Ives - BL to C 74 1
Fareham to Salisbury A 67 3
Faversham to Dover B 05 3
Felixstowe & Aldeburgh - BL to D 20 3
Fenchurch Street to Barking C 20 8
Festiniog - 50 yrs of enterprise C 83 3
Festiniog 1946-55 E 01 7
Festiniog in the Fifties B 68 8
Festiniog in the Sixties B 91 6
Frome to Bristol B 77 0
Fulwell - Trams, Trolleys & Buses D 11 1
G
Gloucester to Bristol D 35 7
Gloucester to Cardiff D 66 1
Gosport & Horndean Trys B 92 3
Gosport - Branch Lines around A 36 9
Great Yarmouth Tramways D 13 5
Greece Narrow Gauge D 72 2
Grimsby & Cleethorpes Trolleybuses D 86 9
H
Hammersmith & Hounslow Trys C 33 8
Hampshire Narrow Gauge D 36 4
Hampstead & Highgate Tramways B 53 4
Harrow to Watford D 14 2
Hastings to Ashford A 37 6
Hastings Tramways B 18 3
Hawkhurst - Branch Line to A 66 6
Hay-on-Wye - Branch Lines around D 92 0
Hayling - Branch Line to A 12 3
Haywards Heath to Seaford A 28 4
Hemel Hempstead - Branch Lines to D 88 3
Henley, Windsor & Marlow - BL to C77 2
Hereford to Newport D 54 8
Hexham to Carlisle D 75 3
Hitchin to Peterborough D 07 4
Holborn & Finsbury Tramways B 79 4
Holborn Viaduct to Lewisham A 81 9
Horsham - Branch Lines to A 02 4
Huddersfield Tramways D 95 1
Huddersfield Trolleybuses C 92 5
Hull Tramways D60 9
Hull Trolleybuses D 24 1
Huntingdon - Branch Lines around A 93 2
I
Ilford & Barking Tramways B 61 9
Ilford to Shenfield C 97 0
Ilfracombe - Branch Line to B 21 3
Ilkeston & Glossop Tramways D 40 1
Index to Middleton Press Stations E 24 6
Industrial Rlys of the South East A 09 3
Ipswich to Saxmundham C 41 3
Ipswich Trolleybuses D 59 3
Isle of Wight Lines - 50 yrs C 12 3
K
Keighley Tramways & Trolleybuses D 83 8
Kent & East Sussex Waterways A 72 X
Kent Narrow Gauge C 45 1
Kent Seaways - Hoys to Hovercraft D 79 1
Kidderminster to Shrewsbury E10 9
Kingsbridge - Branch Line to C 98 7
Kingston & Hounslow Loops A 83 3
Kingston & Wimbledon Tramways B 56 5
Kingswear - Branch Line to C 17 8
L
Lambourn - Branch Line to C 70 3
Launceston & Princetown - BL to C 19 2
Lewisham to Dartford A 92 5
Lines around Wimbledon B 75 6
Liverpool Street to Chingford D 01 2
Liverpool Street to Ilford C 34 5
Liverpool Tramways - Eastern C 04 8
Liverpool Tramways - Northern C 46 8
Liverpool Tramways - Southern C 23 9
Llandudno & Colwyn Bay Tramways E 17 8
London Bridge to Addiscombe B 20 6
London Bridge to East Croydon A 58 1
London Termini - Past and Proposed D 00 5
London to Portsmouth Waterways B 43 5
Longmoor - Branch Lines to A 41 3
Looe - Branch Line to C 22 2
Ludlow to Hereford E 14 7
Lydney - Branch Lines around E 26 0
Lyme Regis - Branch Line to A 45 1
Lynton - Branch Line to B 04 6
M
Maidstone & Chatham Tramways B 40 4
March - Branch Lines around B 09 1
Margate & Ramsgate Tramways C 52 9
Marylebone to Rickmansworth D49 4
Melton Constable to Yarmouth Beach E 03 1
Midhurst - Branch Lines around A 49 9
Military Defence of West Sussex A 23 9
Military Signals, South Coast C 54 3
Mitcham Junction Lines B 01 5
Mitchell & company C 59 8
Monmouth - Branch Lines to E 20 8
Monmouthshire Eastern Valleys D 71 5
Moreton-in-Marsh to Worcester D 26 5
Moretonhampstead - BL to C 27 7
Mountain Ash to Neath D 80 7
N
Newbury to Westbury C 66 6
Newcastle to Hexham D 69 2
Newcastle Trolleybuses D 78 4
Newport (IOW) - Branch Lines to A 26 0
Newquay - Branch Lines to C 71 0
Newton Abbot to Plymouth C 60 4
Northern France Narrow Gauge C 75 8
North East German Narrow Gauge D 44 9
North Kent Tramways B 44 2
North London Line B 94 7
North Woolwich - BLs around C 65 9
Norwich Tramways C 40 6
Nottinghamshire & Derbyshire T/B D 63 0
Nottinghamshire & Derbyshire T/W D 53 1
O
Ongar - Branch Lines to E 05 5
Oxford to Bletchley D57 9
Oxford to Moreton-in-Marsh D 15 9
P
Paddington to Ealing C 37 6
Paddington to Princes Risborough C 81 9
Padstow - Branch Line to B 54 1
Plymouth - BLs around B 98 5
Plymouth to St. Austell C 63 5
Pontypool to Mountain Ash D 65 4
Porthmadog 1954-94 - BL around B 31 2
Portmadoc 1923-46 - BL around B 13 8
Portsmouths Tramways B 72 5
Portsmouth to Southampton A 31 4
Potters Bar to Cambridge D 70 8
Princes Risborough - Branch Lines to D 05 0
Princes Risborough to Banbury C 85 7
R
Reading to Basingstoke B 27 5
Reading to Didcot C 79 6
Reading to Guildford A 47 5
Reading Tramways B 87 9
Reading Trolleybuses C 05 5
Redhill to Ashford A 73 4
Return to Blaenau 1970-82 C 64 2
Rickmansworth to Aylesbury D 61 6
Romania & Bulgaria Narrow Gauge E 23 9
Roman Roads of Hampshire D 67 8
Roman Roads of Kent E 02 4
Roman Roads of Surrey C 61 1
Roman Roads of Sussex C 48 2
Romneyrail C 32 1
Ross-on-Wye - Branch Lines around E 30 7
Ryde to Ventnor A 19 2
S
Salisbury to Westbury B 39 8
Saxmundham to Yarmouth C 69 7
Saxony Narrow Gauge D 47 0
Scarborough Tramways E 15 4
Seaton & Eastbourne Tramways B 76 3
Seaton & Sidmouth - Branch Lines to A
Secret Sussex Resistance B 82 4
Selsey - Branch Line to A 04 8
Shepherds Bush to Uxbridge T/Ws C 2
Shrewsbury - Branch Line to A 86 4
Shrewsbury to Ludlow E 21 5
Shrewsbury to Newtown E 29 1
Sierra Leone Narrow Gauge D 28 9
Sirhowy Valley Line E 12 3
Sittingbourne to Ramsgate A 90 1
Slough to Newbury C 56 7
Solent - Creeks, Crafts & Cargoes D 52
Southamptons Tramways B 33 6
Southampton to Bournemouth A 42 0
Southend-on-Sea Tramways B 28 2
Southern France Narrow Gauge C 47
Southwark & Deptford Tramways B 3
South W Harbours - Ships & Trades E
Southwold - Branch Line to A 15 4
South London Line B 46 6
South London Tramways 1903-33 D 10
South London Tramways 1933-52 D 89
South Shields Trolleybuses E 11 6
St. Albans to Bedford D 08 1
St. Austell to Penzance C 67 3
Stourbridge to Wolverhampton E 16 1
St. Pancras to Barking D 68 5
St. Pancras to St. Albans C 78 9
Stamford Hill Tramways B 85 5
Steaming through the Isle of Wight A 5
Steaming through West Hants A 69 7
Stratford upon avon to Birmingham D
Stratford upon Avon to Cheltenham C
Surrey Home Guard C 57 4
Surrey Narrow Gauge C 87 1
Sussex Home Guard C 24 6
Sussex Narrow Gauge C 68 0
Swanley to Ashford B 45 9
Swindon to Bristol C 96 3
Swindon to Gloucester D46 3
Swindon to Newport D 30 2
Swiss Narrow Gauge C 94 9
T
Talyllyn - 50 years C 39 0
Taunton to Barnstaple B 60 2
Taunton to Exeter C 82 6
Tavistock to Plymouth B 88 6
Tees-side Trolleybuses D 58 6
Tenterden - Branch Line to A 21 5
Three Bridges to Brighton A 35 2
Tilbury Loop C 86 4
Tiverton - Branch Lines around C 62 8
Tivetshall to Beccles D 41 8
Tonbridge to Hastings A 44 4
Torrington - Branch Lines to B 37 4
Tunbridge Wells - Branch Lines to A 3
Twickenham & Kingston Trys C 35 2
U
Upwell - Branch Line to B 64 0
V
Victoria & Lambeth Tramways B 49 7
Victoria to Bromley South A 98 7
Vivarais Revisited E 08 6
W
Walthamstow & Leyton Tramways B
Waltham Cross & Edmonton Trys C 0
Wandsworth & Battersea Tramways
Wantage - Branch Line to D 25 8
Wareham to Swanage - 50 yrs D 09 8
War on the Line A 10 9
Waterloo to Windsor A 54 3
Waterloo to Woking A 38 3
Watford to Leighton Buzzard D 45 6
Wenford Bridge to Fowey C 09 3
Westbury to Bath B 55 8
Westbury to Taunton C 76 5
West Cornwall Mineral Railways D 48
West Croydon to Epsom B 08 4
West German Narrow Gauge D 93 7
West London - Branch Lines of C 50 5
West London Line B 84 8
West Wiltshire - Branch Lines of D 12
Weymouth - Branch Lines around A 6
Willesden Junction to Richmond B 71
Wimbledon to Beckenham C 58 1
Wimbledon to Epsom B 62 6
Wimborne - Branch Lines around A 9
Wisbech - Branch Lines around C 01 7
Wisbech 1800-1901 C 93 2
Woking to Alton A 59 8
Woking to Portsmouth A 25 3
Woking to Southampton A 55 0
Wolverhampton Trolleybuses D 85 2
Woolwich & Dartford Trolleys B 66 4
Worcester to Birmingham D 97 5
Worcester to Hereford D 38 8
Worthing to Chichester A 06 2
Y
Yeovil - 50 yrs change C 38 3
Yeovil to Dorchester A 76 5
Yeovil to Exeter A 91 8
York Tramways & Trolleybuses D 82 1